As one of the world's longest established
and best-known travel brands,
Thomas Cook are the experts in travel.

For more than 135 years our
guidebooks have unlocked the secrets
of destinat⋯⋯⋯world,
⋯⋯th of
⋯⋯avel.

⋯⋯our
⋯⋯trip
⋯⋯ge.

GW00689746

Thomas Cook **pocket** guides

NEW YORK CITY

Your travelling companion since 1873

Thomas
Cook

Written by Randa Bishop
Updated by Andrea M Rotondo

Published by Thomas Cook Publishing
A division of Thomas Cook Tour Operations Limited
Company registration No: 3772199 England
The Thomas Cook Business Park, Unit 9, Coningsby Road,
Peterborough PE3 8SB, United Kingdom
Email: books@thomascook.com, Tel: +44 (0) 1733 416477
www.thomascookpublishing.com

Produced by Cambridge Publishing Management Limited
Burr Elm Court, Main Street, Caldecote CB23 7NU
www.cambridgepm.co.uk

ISBN: 978-1-84848-337-8

© 2006, 2008 Thomas Cook Publishing
This third edition © 2010 Thomas Cook Publishing
Text © Thomas Cook Publishing
Maps © Thomas Cook Publishing/PCGraphics (UK) Limited
Transport map © Communicarta Limited

Project Editor: Karen Beaulah
Production/DTP: Steven Collins

Printed and bound in Spain by GraphyCems

Cover photography © Pictures Colour Library

All rights reserved. No part of this publication may be reproduced, stored in
a retrieval system or transmitted, in any form or by any means, electronic,
mechanical, recording or otherwise, in any part of the world, without prior
permission of the publisher. Requests for permission should be made to
the publisher at the above address.

Although every care has been taken in compiling this publication, and the contents
are believed to be correct at the time of printing, Thomas Cook Tour Operations
Limited cannot accept any responsibility for errors or omissions, however caused,
or for changes in details given in the guidebook, or for the consequences of any
reliance on the information provided. Descriptions and assessments are based on
the author's views and experiences when writing and do not necessarily represent
those of Thomas Cook Tour Operations Limited.

CONTENTS

SYMBOLS KEY

The following symbols are used throughout this book:

ⓐ address ☏ telephone ⓕ fax Ⓦ website address ⓔ email
🕒 opening times Ⓝ public transport connections ❶ important

The following symbols are used on the maps:

𝑖	information office	🚊	railway station
🛫	airport	Ⓜ	metro
➕	hospital	✝	cathedral
🛡	police station	◼	point of interest
🚌	bus station	—	railway
❶	numbers denote featured cafés & restaurants		

Hotels and restaurants are graded by approximate price as follows:
£ = budget price **££** = mid-range price **£££** = expensive

▶ *Aerial view of New York City, Lower Manhattan*

INTRODUCING
New York City

Introduction

New York, formerly New Amsterdam and known variously as The Big Apple and The City That Never Sleeps, has something for everyone: world-class museums, fabulous shopping, a rich art and music scene, theatres galore, premier restaurants, staggering architecture, all-conquering sports teams and ultra-A-list celebrities. But don't let this superlative-drenched city daunt you. Despite its hectic pace and staggering population of 8.25 million, New York is very doable: it's welcoming, easy to navigate and is now one of the safest big cities in the world.

This is a place for which the term 'melting pot' could easily have been coined. From the very beginning, New York has been defined by the vast variety of nationalities that emigrated to America and chose to make the city their home. People came from every nation, every race and every walk of life. They embraced the freedom and opportunity they found in their new land, but they never shed their heritage completely. The people of New York hold tenaciously on to their traditions, and this is what gives the city its flavour. One-time mayor John V Lindsay had it right when he said, 'Not only is New York the nation's melting pot, it is also the casserole, the chafing dish, and the charcoal grill.'

Great leaders built New York on foundations of ambition and courage. Stock and bond trading, started more than 200 years ago by Alexander Hamilton, was the seedling of a world financial centre and a city so populous that its only way to grow was upwards – eventually into a forest of skyscrapers. Mixed in with the urban grandeur you'll find distinct neighbourhoods such as Chinatown, Little Italy, or the Lower East Side with its Hebrew-signed storefronts that are full of unique appeal.

New York has always evolved at a breakneck pace. But increasingly, as working-class enclaves and enticingly seedy areas are swept up in a rising tide of gentrification, residents are wary of losing the character and grit of the city to generic condos and chain stores. Could real estate, long ago acquired for a few beads and trinkets, be the downfall of this international metropolis, as towering glass invaders engulf once-charming neighbourhoods? No way. The people have a passion for their city despite its ever-changing complexion. As O Henry wrote, 'It'll be a great place if they ever finish it!'

🔺 *The Metropolitan Museum*

When to go

Every day of the year is a great day to be in New York. Spring can be thrilling as people emerge from hibernation and parks start to fill. Soaring summer temperatures (see below) tend to send families off to the beaches; consequently, the city is less crowded, and bargains can be found in shops and restaurants. New York wakes up from its summer siesta in September, as horses pound the tracks at Belmont and colourful autumn foliage decorates Central Park. You may need to wrap up for a winter visit, but city festivities will give you the kind of inner glow that renders any thought of having to slide into those thermals entirely redundant.

SEASONS & CLIMATE

The climate does have its swings, but is fairly predictable. Most surprising to visitors is how clear the air is in this dense city. Late spring is very pleasant, with temperatures reaching 25°C (77°F) by June. Freshness gives way to summer's hot and humid weather in July and August, when temperatures can hit an average high of 28°C (83°F). The weather can be balmy right up to November, but when stormy winds move in, expect snow. New York can be crystal clear, yet brutally cold, with wind chill lowering the average temperature to around 2°C (36°F).

ANNUAL EVENTS
January & February

New Year's Eve As the Times Square giant ball drops at the stroke of midnight, one million people welcome in the New Year.
ⓦ www.timessquarenyc.org

Chinese New Year (3 Feb 2011; 23 Feb 2012) Processions of lion dancers in

Chinatown are accompanied by clashing cymbals, gongs and drums.
ⓐ Festivities centre on Mott St ⓦ www.betterchinatown.com

March & April
St Patrick's Day Parade (17 Mar) Bagpipers play and marching bands
parade along Fifth Avenue. ⓣ (212) 484 1222 ⓦ www.nyc.gov or
ⓦ www.saintpatricksdayparade.com
Easter Parade (24 Apr 2011; 8 Apr 2012) Spring strollers display
imaginative, sometimes flamboyant and occasionally terrifying
bonnets. ⓐ Fifth Ave, 49th to 57th Sts

May
Cherry Blossom Festival Brooklyn Botanic Garden's (see page 132)
celebration comes at the height of the cherry blossom season.
ⓦ www.bbg.org
Fleet Week (late May) Military ships parade up the Hudson River,
and there is a formation flyover.

🔺 *The Greek Independence Day parade on Fifth Avenue*

Ninth Avenue International Food Festival (late May) A spread of food delicacies extending from 37th to 57th Streets on Ninth Avenue. ⑦ (212) 581 7217 ⓦ www.ninthavenuefoodfestival.com

June & July
The New York Lesbian & Gay Film Festival A ten-day, pink-tinged cine-fest. ⑦ (212) 571 2170 ⓦ www.newfest.org

Museum Mile Festival Nine museums offer free admission (see page 18). ⓐ Fifth Ave, between 82nd & 105th Sts ⑦ (212) 606 2296 ⓦ www.museummilefestival.org

Midsummer Night Swing Big bands let rip at an outdoor dance party at Lincoln Center's Fountain Plaza (see page 100). ⓦ www.lincolncenter.org

Macy's 4th of July Fireworks Displays fly in the sky over the East River. ⑦ (212) 494 4495

August
Lincoln Center Out of Doors A month of music and dance. ⓦ www.lincolncenter.org

September & October
Howl! Festival Days of music and theatre, including Wigstock, a drag queen show. ⓐ Thompkins Sq Park ⓦ www.howlfestival.com

Harlem Week Month-long Hispanic and black cultural event with food, music and a film festival. ⑦ (212) 862 7200 ⓦ www.harlemdiscover.com

Feast of San Gennaro Little Italy's feast honours the patron saint of Naples. ⓐ Mulberry St ⓦ www.sangennaro.org

New York Film Festival Beginning the last Friday in September, the 17-day festival showcases emerging talent at the Lincoln Center (see page 100). ⑦ Box office: (212) 875 5050 ⓦ www.filmlinc.com

Greenwich Village Halloween Parade Delightful night-time parade.

Join in – you know you want to. ⓐ Sixth Ave from Spring St to 23rd St
ⓦ www.halloween-nyc.com

November & December
New York City Marathon The five-borough, 42-km (26-mile) run starts in
Staten Island and finishes in Central Park (see page 12). ⓦ www.nyrr.org
Macy's Thanksgiving Day Parade (commences 09.00, fourth Thur in
Nov) Enormous helium-filled balloons float over Central Park West.
ⓐ 77th St & Central Park West to Columbus Circle down Broadway
to Herald Sq ❶ (212) 494 4495
Christmas Tree Lighting Ceremony A tree glitters with 30,000 bulbs
at the Rockefeller Center (see page 62). ❶ (212) 632 3975
Christmas Windows Fifth Avenue stores display creatively dressed
holiday windows.

PUBLIC HOLIDAYS	
New Year's Day	1 Jan
Martin Luther King Day	17 Jan 2011, 16 Jan 2012, 21 Jan 2013
President's Day	21 Feb 2011; 20 Feb 2012; 18 Feb 2013
Easter Sunday	24 Apr 2011; 8 Apr 2012; 31 March 2013
Memorial Day	30 May 2011; 28 May 2012; 27 May 2013
Independence Day	4 July
Labor Day	5 Sept 2011; 3 Sept 2012; 2 Sept 2013
Columbus Day	10 Oct 2011; 8 Oct 2012; 14 Oct 2013
Veterans' Day	11 Nov
Thanksgiving Day	24 Nov 2011; 22 Nov 2012; 28 Nov 2013
Hanukkah commences	21 Dec 2011; 9 Dec 2012; 28 Nov 2013
Christmas Day	25 Dec

Central Park: an urban oasis

No trip to New York City is complete without a visit to the magnificent, much-loved Central Park. Set between Fifth and Eighth (Central Park West) Avenues and stretching from 59th Street (Central Park South) up to 110th Street, the 341-hectare (843-acre) green space has been something of a refuge for city dwellers since its very earliest days. Surprisingly, the park started as a swamp. More than 150 years ago, Frederick Law Olmsted converted an area of waterlogged marshland into a pastoral park for the citizens of what was then lower Manhattan. By the early 1900s, it contained many of the attractions that are still found today, including – take a deep breath – the zoo, children's playgrounds, lakes, a huge reservoir, sculptures, fountains, ball fields, a carousel, an ice-skating rink and several cafés.

Over the years, the park has appeared in some 200 films, welcomed fans paying homage to John Lennon at Strawberry Fields and been the scene of countless marriage proposals. Its inviting nooks, dappled walking paths and immense open spaces constantly draw the crowds. Whether explored on foot, bike, rowing boat or horse-drawn carriage, the park is a delight in any season; but in spring it blooms gloriously. The **Central Park Conservancy**'s free guided walking tours (ⓦ www.centralparknyc.org) are a great way to see it at its best – rain or shine. If you're feeling romantic – and who wouldn't be in this picturesque environment? – opt for a carriage ride with **Central Park Carriages** (ⓐ Central Park South (59th St) between Fifth & Sixth Aves ⓣ (212) 736 0680 ⓦ www.centralparkcarriages.com).

From May to Labor Day, the park becomes a sanctuary of the arts where you can enjoy an evening of free music or theatre surrounded by American elms and a backdrop of skyscrapers. In autumn you could rent a rowing boat and take in the foliage from the water, then enjoy a cocktail, lunch or dinner lakeside at the **Loeb Boathouse** (② E 72nd St & Park Drive North ① (212) 517 2233 ⓦ www.thecentralparkboathouse.com). In winter, get your skates on and have a night under the stars at Trump Wollman Rink (see page 31).

So: culture – check; romance – check; splendour – check. Check out Central Park.

▲ *Central Park is New York's oasis of green and calm*

History

For thousands of years, Algonquin Lenape Native Americans inhabited the area around what's now known as the Hudson River. The first foreigner to arrive, leading French explorers in 1554, was Giovanni da Verrazano. Fifty-five years later, ignoring the route commissioned by the Dutch, British captain Henry Hudson came upon New York by chance when he sailed into the harbour in September 1609. In 1624, Governor's Island was settled as a Dutch trading post and two years later Dutch-born Peter Minuit acquired Manhattan Island (a Lenape name) for the legendary sum of $24-worth of beads.

James, Duke of York, brother to King Charles II, asserted the British claim to the area in 1664, when British warships arrived and, without a shot fired, took New Amsterdam and renamed it New York (after the duke). During the American Revolution, which began in 1775, George Washington waged war to defend New York, but, after heavy losses, retreated. In 1783 he returned, marching into Manhattan to claim victory. From 1783 to 1790 New York was the US capital, and Washington's inauguration as the country's first president took place on 30 April 1789 at Federal Hall on Wall Street (see page 79).

The city soon became a leading financial and shipping centre, with the Buttonwood Agreement of 1792 leading to the development of the New York Stock Exchange in the early 1800s and the opening of the Erie Canal in 1825. The Statue of Liberty (see page 77), a gift from the people of France, was unveiled in 1886 and greeted immigrants arriving at Ellis Island (see page 77). Bridges and tunnels were built connecting Manhattan with Brooklyn, Queens, Staten Island and the Bronx, and by 1898 these outer boroughs officially became part of New York City.

The first half of the 20th century was an era of continued growth. The first subway opened in 1904 and, even in the face of the Great Depression, New York's skyline rose to new heights with the Chrysler Building (see page 58) and Empire State Building (see page 64). During the 1970s, crime-ridden, facing bankruptcy and hampered by a decaying infrastructure, New York developed a notorious reputation that bled into the 1980s. But by the mid-1990s, determined efforts to revitalise the city prevailed. Crime rates fell and tourism flourished.

Through booms and busts, the city has forged ahead. The attacks on the World Trade Center on 11 September 2001 left an indelible scar, however. The city was forced to come to terms with the fact that it had changed irrevocably in the space of one spectacularly bloody morning. Its inhabitants' determination to get back to business as usual as quickly as possible typified New Yorkers. New York City continues to evolve despite the global recession and state and city deficits. City leaders, including Mayor Michael Bloomberg, are finding ways to do more with less to keep the city shining.

◆ *The Stock Exchange building*

Lifestyle

As the early-morning crowds fuss their way across the avenues of midtown Manhattan, one question forms itself in the visitor's astonished mind: where on earth is everybody rushing to? A lot of them are going to work. On weekdays, when workers and visitors fill up the city, Manhattan's population increases sevenfold from its resident base of 1.5 million – that's a mass of 10.5 million on the move! New Yorkers go about their business come rain or shine, and they don't hang about – hence the out-of-towners' phrase, 'a New York minute', a temporal measurement spanning about ten seconds! It's accurate to say that patience is not universally regarded as a cardinal virtue in this city.

New Yorkers work hard, but they also make the most of their leisure time: inhabitants appreciate the varied eateries, boutiques, nightlife and neighbourhoods. They are inquisitive and enthusiastic, savvy and stylish. The same Cro-Magnon commuter who'd think nothing of having you whacked for stepping in his way on a Friday morning is, come the evening, a cultured metrosexual, a humanitarian, an aesthete. As comfortable in a suit as in blue jeans, they'll enjoy a pretzel from a street vendor alfresco in the morning and dine on caviar at night. New Yorkers are a relatively unfazable lot, absorbing bewildering experiences – from withstanding sardine-like conditions on subway cars during rush hour to politely trying to feign shock at the antics of attention-seeking flashers – as normal occurrences in everyday big-city life.

When it comes to going out, weekends and weekdays blend into one. Bars and restaurants are full every day of the week. It is, after all, the city that never sleeps.

Immerse yourself in New York street life at night

Culture

Culture? Are you kidding? You can't move for it, from sponsored initiatives to the summer line-up at Central Park (see page 12) – a cultural programme in itself. The city's founders helped to establish it as an arts capital, and consequently there are museums and galleries in every neighbourhood, as the listings for the city areas in this guide demonstrate. And then there's Broadway, with 40 theatres around Times Square (see page 60) and the Off-Broadway and Off-Off-Broadway venues in Greenwich Village and SoHo.

The free and eclectic *Village Voice* has comprehensive listings of what's going on around the city, as do *Time Out New York*, *The New Yorker* and *New York* magazine. Oh, and did we mention the museums?

MUSEUM MILE

There are nine museums along this famous Fifth Avenue mile, running downtown from 104th Street. Here they are, listed as the traffic flows:

- **El Museo del Barrio** Dedicated to Puerto Rican, Caribbean and Latin American art. ⓐ 1230 Fifth Ave at 104th St ① (212) 831 7272 ⓦ www.elmuseo.org ① 11.00–18.00 Tues–Sun, closed Mon ⓝ Subway: 6 to 103rd St; 2, 3 to Central Park North ① Admission charge

- **Museum of the City of New York** Explores the past, present and future of the city. ⓐ 1220 Fifth Ave at 103rd St ① (212) 534 1672 ⓦ www.mcny.org ① 10.00–17.00 Tues–Sun, closed Mon ⓝ Subway: 2, 3 to 110th St ① Admission charge

⬥ *Amazing Guggenheim Museum central atrium*

- **The Jewish Museum** Jewish culture and art. ⓐ 1109 Fifth Ave at 92nd St ⓣ (212) 423 3200 ⓦ www.thejewishmuseum.org ⓛ 11.00–17.45 Sat–Tues, 11.00–20.00 Thur, closed Wed & Fri ⓝ Subway: 4, 5, 6 to 86th St ⓘ Admission charge
- **Cooper-Hewitt National Design Museum, Smithsonian Institution** (see page 87)
- **National Academy Museum and School of Fine Arts** Two centuries of American art are on display. ⓐ 1083 Fifth Ave at 89th St ⓣ (212) 369 4880 ⓦ www.nationalacademy.org ⓛ 12.00–17.00 Wed & Thur, 13.00–21.00 Fri, 11.00–18.00 Sat & Sun, closed Mon & Tues ⓝ Subway: 4, 5, 6 to 86th St ⓘ Admission charge
- **Solomon R. Guggenheim Museum** (see page 88)
- **Neue Galerie New York** German and Austrian art and design. ⓐ 1048 Fifth Ave at 86th St ⓣ (212) 628 6200 ⓦ www.neuegalerie.org ⓛ 11.00–18.00 Thur–Mon, closed Tues & Wed ⓝ Subway: 4, 5, 6 to 86th St ⓘ Admission charge
- **Goethe-Institut New York/German Cultural Center** A tremendously cultural centre. ⓐ 1014 Fifth Ave at 83rd St ⓣ (212) 439 8700 ⓦ www.goethe.de/newyork ⓔ info@newyork.goethe.org ⓝ Subway: 4, 5, 6 to 86th St
- **The Metropolitan Museum of Art** (see page 88)

ⓓ *Broadway, Fifth Avenue and 23rd Street meet in front of the Flatiron Building*

MAKING THE MOST OF
New York City

Shopping

The shopping scene in New York is tremendously seductive. For starters, there's **Macy's** (🅐 151 W 34th St 🅣 (212) 695 4400 🅦 www.macys.com 🅛 10.00–20.30 Mon–Sat, 11.00–19.00 Sun), a block-long department store selling everything from cosmetics and clothes to food delicacies and household goods, as well as other shopping institutions such as Bloomingdales (see page 91) and **Saks Fifth Avenue** (🅐 611 Fifth Ave 🅣 (212) 753 4000 🅦 www.saksfifthavenue.com 🅛 10.00–20.00 Mon–Sat, 12.00–19.00 Sun).

Looking like a Paris fashion catwalk, Madison Avenue above 50th Street is home to very expensive designer boutiques. Fashionistas will also want to explore every block of SoHo (South

---

'I CAN GET IT FOR YOU WHOLESALE'

This is a New York expression as old as the city, and indulging in a spot of retail therapy certainly doesn't mean breaking the bank. Try some of these for size: at **Century 21** (🅐 22 Cortlandt St 🅣 (212) 227 9092 🅦 www.c21stores.com 🅛 07.45–21.00 Mon–Wed, 07.45–21.30 Thur & Fri, 10.00–21.00 Sat, 11.00–20.00 Sun) you'll pick up family clothing at somewhere between 25 and 75 per cent off; **INA** (🅐 101 Thompson St 🅣 (212) 941 4757 🅛 12.00–19.00 Sun–Thur, 12.00–20.00 Fri & Sat 🅦 www.inanyc.com) knocks out designer men's and women's handbags, jeans and dresses at low prices. Every Sunday sees Orchard Street closed to traffic on Orchard from Delancey to East Houston so that businesses can sell their wares on the pavement.

of Houston), Bleecker Street in the West Village and the shops tucked in along the main drag in the Meatpacking District. For less pricey finds, head to NoHo (North of Houston) and the Lower East Side.

In Harlem, check out the **Malcolm Shabazz Harlem Market** (📍 52 W 116th St ☎ (212) 987 8131 🕐 10.00–20.00) for traditional African crafts and textiles.

Museum gift shops have some of the more eclectic buys in the city. Jazz collectors, DJs and other music lovers will want to hit the record stores in Greenwich Village (see page 104), and wine lovers can stock up at **Astor Wine & Spirits** (📍 399 Lafayette St ☎ (212) 674 7500 🌐 www.astorwines.com). Keep an eye out for street vendors and weekend flea markets, ideal for random finds, from jewellery to vintage clothes to organic foodstuffs to pottery.

⬤ *Macy's is every shopper's paradise*

Eating & drinking

New York is a foodie's paradise. Whether you're looking to sample
celebrity chefs' latest creations or simply craving the basics,
choosing where to go and possibly landing a reservation are
the only things standing in your way. The city is graced with
20,000 eating establishments, not counting street vendors, bars
and cafés. You can find a delicious dish at any price range to fit
every mood. Does Thai, Turkish or Ethiopian sound enticing?
Perhaps Korean, Moroccan or Brazilian?

Restaurants with prestigious reputations can be ruthlessly
expensive. But nowadays famous chefs are reaching out to
a broader public with informal restaurants in emerging
neighbourhoods. The new eateries emphasise quality menus,
and some of them are amazingly reasonable. New Yorkers order
an entrée (main course) and salad, often skipping appetisers,
desserts and coffee unless they're out for a special evening.
Portions tend to be large and include a complement of vegetables.
An entrée-only meal means you can eat haute cuisine and not
break the bank.

Look for California wines on the menu: Napa Valley's aromatic
Cabernet Sauvignon, or Pinot Noir and Chardonnay from Sonoma
are reliable options. Try Robert Mondavi's Stag's Leap, or Kendall

PRICE CATEGORIES

The restaurant price guides given in this book indicate
the approximate cost of a main dish without drinks:
£ = up to $25   ££ = $25–46   £££ = over $46

Jackson. Some restaurants are BYOB (bring your own bottle), allowing guests to bring their own alcoholic beverage – generally wine or beer only, with a nominal corkage fee.

◆ *Delmonico's Restaurant, since 1837*

Locals do their fair share of eating on the run. Ubiquitous delis offer a wide variety of freshly made breakfast sandwiches and lunch items. And what would New York do without its pizza joints? Order a slice for a quick lunch. Bagels with cream cheese (and salmon lox!) are another favourite. Hot dogs and hamburgers are also traditional standbys.

Open-air markets, where regional growers sell fresh produce and other goods, can be found year-round. The largest, at Union Square, is open Monday, Wednesday, Friday and Saturday from 08.00 until 18.00. It's a great place to meet locals and to forage for picnic ingredients such as freshly baked breads, local honey and just-ripe fruits. Supermarkets **Zabars** (ⓐ 2245 Broadway at 80th St ① (212) 787 2000 ⓦ www.zabars.com ⓛ 08.00–19.30 Mon–Fri, 08.00–20.00 Sat, 09.00–18.00 Sun) and **Whole Foods** (ⓐ 10 Columbus Circle ① (212) 823 9600 ⓦ www.wholefoods.com ⓛ 08.00–23.00 ⓝ Subway: A, B, C, D, 1 to 59th St–Columbus Circle) offer extensive upmarket prepared foods that are also perfect for picnics.

Bars and lounges are abundant and hot. Some stay open until dawn and offer libations with enticing names. Beers from local brewers Brooklyn Brewery and Six Point Craft Ale, among others, can be found on tap across the city. Not into alcohol? Try a smoothie or a speciality coffee at one of many cafés. A good time to visit is during Restaurant Week, a biennial event (odd years) held in July. Fine restaurants and notable chefs offer *prix fixe* menus.

In general, restaurants' lunch hours are 11.00–15.00, and dinner usually 17.00–23.00.

The most popular places are sometimes reserved months in advance, so if you can't get in for dinner, try for lunch. In most restaurants, you won't ever have to ask for the bill (or 'check'), as servers have a habit of bringing it to the table once entrée plates are cleared if no other food is ordered. Credit cards are accepted in most larger restaurants, though smaller establishments often only take cash. To lighten the burden, check online for discount coupons (ⓦ www.restaurant.com). Tax is extra, plus customary gratuities (15–20 per cent) – just double the tax to work out the tip. Tipping is usually up to the customer, but for larger parties it can be mandatory (in which case it will be stated on the menu).

Smoking is banned in New York City bars and restaurants.

◗ Some of New York's most popular fast food

Entertainment & nightlife

Simply put, New York is at both the cutting-edge and the global crossroads of entertainment – from house to hip hop, from samba to salsa – and beyond. Music is everywhere. It bursts from passing boom boxes on sidewalks, soulful trumpets toot underground on a subway platform, and techno rips all night long at the clubs.

The 1920s Harlem Renaissance filled Big Apple clubs with jazz and blues and with performers like Louis Armstrong and Count Basie. Visitors can reminisce about the era today at the Apollo Theater (see page 98). The venue that launched such music greats as Ella Fitzgerald and Michael Jackson still showcases new talent.

Making people laugh is the goal of improvisational comedians at Chelsea's wacky **Upright Citizens Brigade Theatre** (📍 307 W 26th St ☎ (212) 366 9176 🌐 www.ucbtheatre.com) and in Times Square (see page 60). Broadway theatre has been booming ever since the sleaze around Times Square was cleaned up during the 1990s. There's a renaissance of Tin Pan Alley pop and Broadway musicals in small café-society cabaret venues all around the city.

The demise of cavernous disco palace Studio 54 really led to the end of that type of place in the city, full stop. These days, high-calibre, night-owl DJs spin records to the wee hours, dishing out IDM, straight-up techno, microhouse, hip hop, drum 'n' bass, or punk in clubs that come and go like waves. Many are in trendy neighbourhoods like Chelsea, the Meatpacking District and SoHo. Getting past the velvet rope may require a charm school degree; go on weekdays when hip New Yorkers go out, and expect to pay the bill with cash.

Check the web at 🌐 www.newyork.timeout.com for up-to-date information and listings for nightclubs, lounges and parties.

A few tips: have ID to hand – not your passport – even if you're over 40; be nice to the doorman; what you wear really matters; go on a weekday as at weekends the clubs will be very crowded; prepare for a pricey night. Bring cash and take a cab home.

🔺 Queuing for theatre tickets in Times Square

Sport & relaxation

SPECTATOR SPORTS

New Yorkers worship their home teams, starting with the
purveyors of the national sport – baseball. The Yankees play at
Yankee Stadium in the Bronx (ⓐ 161st St & River Ave ① (718) 293
6000 ⓦ www.yankees.mlb.com). The Mets play at **Citi Field** at Willets
Point in Queens (ⓐ 123 Roosevelt Ave ① (718) 507 TIXX
ⓦ www.mets.mlb.com). **Madison Square Garden** (ⓐ Seventh Ave &
32nd St ① (212) 465 6741 ⓦ www.thegarden.com) hosts the Knicks
basketball team, as well as ice hockey's Rangers. American football

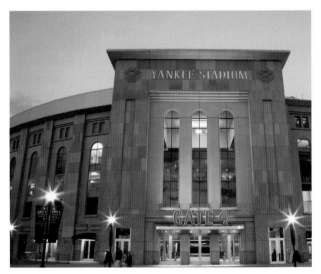

● *Yankees' home in the Bronx*

fans can catch the 2008 Superbowl champions, the New York Giants at **Giants Stadium** in Meadowlands' Sports Complex (🅔 Stadium Rd & W Peripheral Rd ❶ (201) 935 8500 🆆 www.giants.com), across the Hudson River in New Jersey.

The **US Tennis Open** (late Aug–mid-Sept 🆆 www.usopen.org) is played at the **USTA Billie Jean King National Tennis Center** (🄰 Flushing Meadows Corona Park 🆆 www.usta.com), located in Queens.

PARTICIPATION SPORTS

Central Park (see page 12) is Manhattan's back yard. Joggers run around the soft-surface reservoir track while cyclists circle the entire park on three wide paths. Boats, bikes and Rollerblades can all be hired in the park.

Wall climbing is available at **North Meadow Recreation Center** (❶ (212) 348 4867 🕒 10.00–20.00 Mon–Fri, 10.00–18.00 Sat & Sun). Come the first snowfall, locals brush the dust off their skis and go cross-country skiing in Sheep Meadow or on the Great Lawn, while ice-skating is available at **Trump Wollman Rink** (🅔 Near Central Park South–59th St & 6th Ave ❶ (212) 439 6900).

RELAXATION

Along the waterfront, the Hudson River Park jogging path extends all the way from Battery Park (see page 76) to the George Washington Bridge (see page 94). Spend a day sailing with **Come Sail New York!** (🅔 Liberty Landing, Jersey City, NJ ❶ (201) 887 8700 🆆 www.sailthehudson.com). At **Chelsea Piers** (🅔 23rd St & the Hudson River ❶ (212) 336 6666 🆆 www.chelseapiers.com) you'll find a health spa and golf driving range. If pure, unalloyed fear relaxes you, try your hand at some high flying at the **New York Trapeze School** (🅔 Pier 40 on West St at Houston St ❶ (212) 242 8769 🆆 www.newyork.trapezeschool.com).

Accommodation

While there are many hotels in New York, finding affordable, available rooms can be daunting. The solution is to book several months in advance, visit in January or July (but you'll have to reckon with the weather) or opt to stay uptown or in nearby Brooklyn (see page 132). Be sure to look for and ask about special deals (such as at weekends). It's very possible to rest your head for a dreamy sleep in a bunk bed (dreamy, because you're paying $50 or less for the night). Yet if splurging is your goal, you'll find hotels that offer iPod docking stations, Bulgari bath amenities and similar luxuries.

There are plenty of chain hotels around the city with reasonable rates. The hotels listed here are a combination of economic hostels, budget hotels with charm (these may have shared bathrooms), and standard and boutique hotels in neighbourhoods all over Manhattan.

HOTELS

Americana Inn £ Great Times Square location. This small hotel provides a mini-sink in each room, shared bathroom and kitchenette. ❸ 69 W 38th St ❶ (212) 840 6700 ❺ (212) 840 1830 ❽ www.newyorkhotel.com ❽ Subway: B, D, F, M to 42nd St

PRICE CATEGORIES

The following price guides are based on the cost of a room for two people per night. Room tax and breakfast are not included in price unless indicated. Please note rates can fluctuate based on day, season and availability.

£ = up to $175   **££** = $175–300   **£££** = over $300

Gershwin Hotel £ This Tin Pan Alley Greek Revival hotel/hostel has its accent on pop art, and lots of fun. **ⓐ** 7 E 27th St **ⓣ** (212) 545 8000 **ⓕ** (212) 684 5546 **ⓦ** www.gershwinhotel.com **Ⓝ** Subway: N, R, 6 to 28th St

Larchmont Hotel £ A small beaux arts town house fits right into the Village. Shared bathrooms and continental breakfasts. **ⓐ** 27 W 11th St **ⓣ** (212) 989 9333 **ⓕ** (212) 989 9496 **ⓦ** www.larchmonthotel.com **Ⓝ** Subway: F, N, R, M to 14th St

🔺 *The Gershwin Hotel is truly a unique place to stay*

Hotel Belleclaire £–££ A landmark hotel near Lincoln Center, it provides goose-down comforters, no less. Some rooms have shared bathrooms. ⓐ 250 W 77th St ⓣ (212) 362 7700 ⓕ (212) 362 1004 ⓦ www.hotelbelleclaire.com ⓝ Subway: 1 to 79th St

Chelsea Pines Inn ££ Expect neat rooms and old-school Hollywood posters in this gay-owned guesthouse between Chelsea and Greenwich Village. Wi-Fi and continental breakfast are included in rates. ⓐ 317 W 14th St ⓣ (212) 929 1023 ⓦ www.chelseapinesinn.com ⓝ Subway: A, C, E, L to 14th St–Eighth Ave

Hotel Edison ££ This large Art Deco hotel has giant wall murals in the lobby and is next to Times Square. ⓐ 228 W 47th St ⓣ (212) 840 5000 ⓕ (212) 596 6850 ⓦ www.edisonhotelnyc.com ⓝ Subway: N, R to 49th St; B, D, F, M to 47th–50th Sts–Rockefeller Center

Hotel Pennsylvania ££ This huge hotel saw glory in the jazz days; now it's economical and well located. ⓐ 401 Seventh Ave ⓣ (212) 736 5000 ⓕ (212) 502 8712 ⓦ www.hotelpenn.com ⓝ Subway: 1, 2, 3 to 34th St–Penn Station

Off-Soho Suites ££ Two-guest and four-guest suites have private baths and kitchens. There are workout facilities and Wi-Fi access in the lobby. ⓐ 11 Rivington St ⓣ (212) 979 9808 ⓦ www.offsoho.com ⓝ Subway: J, M, Z to Bowery; F to Second Ave; B, D to Grand St

The SoHoTel ££ Good value in NoLita (North of Little Italy); small rooms, most with private bathroom; an upgrade secures vaulted ceilings. ⓐ 341 Broome St ⓣ (212) 226 1482 ⓕ (212) 226 3525 ⓦ www.sohotel-ny.com ⓝ Subway: B, D to Grand St; J, M, Z to Bowery

Washington Square Hotel ££ Once a haven for artists, the hotel has a comfy bar, fab rooms and free breakfast. ❷ 103 Waverly Pl ❶ (212) 777 9515 ❶ (212) 979 8373 Ⓦ www.wshotel.com Ⓝ Subway: A, B, C, D, E, F, M 4th St

Hudson Hotel ££–£££ Decorated in daring colours, this hotel with tiny rooms boasts trendy clientele and a roof terrace. ❷ 356 W 58th St ❶ (212) 554 6000 ❶ (212) 554 6001 Ⓦ www.hudsonhotel.com Ⓝ Subway: A, B, C, D, 1 to 59th St– Columbus Circle

Hotel Thirty Thirty ££–£££ Situated on a quiet street in the Murray Hill area, this renovated hotel is quite affordable. ❷ 30 E 30th St ❶ (212) 689 1900 ❶ (212) 689 0023 Ⓦ www.thirtythirty-nyc.com Ⓝ Subway: 6 to 28th St

Room Mate Grace ££–£££ Swim in the lobby pool, a stylish adjunct to Wi-Fi access and flat-screen TVs in each room. ❷ 125 W 45th St ❶ (212) 354 2323 ❶ (212) 308 8585 Ⓦ www.room-matehotels.com Ⓝ Subway: B, D, F, M to 47th–50th Sts–Rockefeller Center

60 Thompson £££ A designer hotel in SoHo with a chic mood, a guest-only rooftop, modern rooms and down duvets. ❷ 60 Thompson St ❶ (212) 431 0400 ❶ (212) 431 0200 Ⓦ www.60thompson.com Ⓝ Subway: C, E to Spring St

Gansevoort £££ This towering hotel has full-service luxury in the Meatpacking District. Relax in the roof garden pool. ❷ 18 Ninth Ave ❶ (212) 206 6700 ❶ (212) 255 5858 Ⓦ www.hotelgansevoort.com Ⓝ Subway: A, C, E, L to 14th St

Gramercy Park Hotel £££ Funky and de luxe, this hotel pays homage to its haute-bohemian roots. Rooms feature pieces by artists such as Andy Warhol, Jean-Michel Basquiat and Keith Haring. **ⓐ** 2 Lexington Ave **ⓣ** (212) 920 3300 **ⓦ** www.gramercyparkhotel.com **Ⓝ** Subway: 6, N, R to 23rd St

Library Hotel £££ This luxury boutique hotel has a poetry garden; knock out a couple of stanzas over afternoon tea. **ⓐ** 299 Madison Ave **ⓣ** (212) 983 4500 **ⓕ** (212) 499 9099 **ⓦ** www.libraryhotel.com **Ⓝ** Subway: S, 4, 5, 6, 7 to 42nd St–Grand Central

The Lowell £££ An ultra-luxury boutique hotel on the Upper East Side that provides suites with working fireplaces, Bulgari amenities and a regal afternoon tea in the Pembroke Room. **ⓐ** 28 E 63rd St **ⓣ** (212) 838 1400 **ⓕ** (212) 319 4230 **ⓦ** www.lowellhotel.com **Ⓝ** Subway: F to Lexington Ave–63rd St

On the Avenue £££ Close to the Lincoln Center, with charming, stylish rooms. There's a viewing balcony exclusive to guests. **ⓐ** 2178 Broadway **ⓣ** (212) 362 1100 **ⓕ** (212) 787 9521 **ⓦ** www.ontheave-nyc.com **Ⓝ** Subway: 1 to 79th St

Waldorf-Astoria £££ This landmark hotel gave the world Waldorf Salad. **ⓐ** 301 Park Ave **ⓣ** (212) 355 3000 **ⓕ** (212) 872 7272 **ⓦ** www.waldorf.com **Ⓝ** Subway: 6 to 51st St

HOSTELS
Chelsea International Hostel £ This hostel provides sheets and has an Internet café. **ⓐ** 251 W 20th St **ⓣ** (212) 647 0010 **ⓕ** (212) 727 7289 **ⓦ** www.chelseahostel.com **Ⓝ** Subway: C, E to 23rd St

Hostelling International New York £ On the Upper West Side, this large hostel organises good walking tours. ⓐ 891 Amsterdam Ave ⓣ (212) 932 2300 ⓕ (212) 932 2574 ⓦ www.hinewyork.org ⓝ Subway: 1 to 103rd St

Jazz on the Town £ This Union Square location is one of five in Manhattan run by Jazz Hostels. ⓐ 307 E 14th St ⓣ (212) 228 2780 ⓦ www.jazzhostels.com ⓝ Subway: L, N, Q, R, 4, 5, 6 to 14th St–Union Sq

Vanderbilt YMCA £ Steps from the United Nations, the 'Y' is well located for tourist sites. All rooms have TV. ⓐ 224 E 47th St (also located in Harlem, West Side, Brooklyn) ⓣ (212) 756 9600 ⓕ (212) 752 0210 ⓦ www.ymcanyc.org ⓝ Subway: 6 to 51st St

▲ *The Waldorf is a New York icon*

THE BEST OF NEW YORK CITY

Some people visit New York in a mad dash, but, if you're wise, you'll linger longer in this wonderful city. There is so much on offer, it's hard to choose what to do. But there are some places that should not be missed.

TOP 10 ATTRACTIONS

- **Eclectic neighbourhoods** The hip and happening areas that keep the city fresh are in a constant state of exciting evolution (see page 118).

- **Empire State Building** You don't need to be King – or Queen – Kong to appreciate the spectacular city views given by this iconic skyscraper (see page 64).

- **Broadway (& Times Square)** A huge variety of top-class productions ensures that the most famous theatre district in the world constantly renews its dramatic licence (see page 60).

- **Lincoln Center** The world's finest young musicians, wackiest clowns and most wonderful warblers make this a pitch-perfect crucible of performing arts magic (see page 100).

- **Museum Mile** – count them! – top-of-the-range museums in a row (see page 18).

- **Central Park** This blueprint for a city park is an unrivalled cornucopia of delights (see page 12).

- **Rockefeller Center** You could easily spend a fortnight or two in this Art Deco, rinky-dink world of its own (see page 62).

- **Statue of Liberty** The sight that sparked hope in millions of new arrivals still represents what New Yorkers value most in the world (see page 77).

- **Brooklyn Bridge** This New York icon lets you get from Manhattan to Brooklyn without donning a swimsuit (see page 132).

- **Wall Street** From George Washington to Gordon Gekko and far, far beyond, this 9/11 survivor is coming back atcha (see page 79).

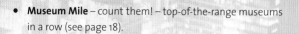 *The unmistakable vista of New York at night*

Suggested itineraries

HALF-DAY: NEW YORK CITY IN A HURRY

Start off at Rockefeller Plaza, then walk west, passing Radio City
Music Hall (see page 73), to witness Times Square (see page 60).
Then hop on the subway (N or R) at 42nd Street to 34th Street to see
the Empire State Building (see page 64) and at least peek in the Art
Deco lobby. After that, continue downtown on the train (R) to the
Prince Street stop in SoHo.

If there's time, jump back on the subway down to the end of
town. The Statue of Liberty (see page 77) is visible from Battery Park
(see page 76).

1 DAY: TIME TO SEE A LITTLE MORE

Consider the above half-day itinerary, but start on the free, half-hour
Staten Island Ferry for a closer look at Ellis Island and the famous
Statue of Liberty (see page 77). Alternatively, take the **Circle Line**
(ⓐ Pier 83, W 42nd St & Twelfth Ave ⓣ (212) 563 3200
ⓦ www.circleline42.com) for a two-hour cruise that skirts around
half of Manhattan. Spend some time in the museum of your choice,
perhaps the Museum of Modern Art (see page 66), on your way up
Fifth Avenue. Eat a hot dog on the run before exploring the twisty
streets of Greenwich Village, Chinatown, Chelsea or the Lower East
Side. In the evening, dine with locals or listen to some jazz.

2–3 DAYS: TIME TO SEE MUCH MORE

Buy a CityPass (see page 43), which covers entry to several sights,
and consider the hop-on, hop-off Gray Line's (see page 56) loop tours
that run the length of Manhattan. Watch the city light up from the
Brooklyn Bridge (see page 132). Explore more neighbourhoods, and

take a walk in Central Park (see page 12). Visit the United Nations (see page 63) or the New Museum (see page 123) and sample cuisines from around the world. Marvel at the medieval collection at The Cloisters (see page 98), before seeing a theatre performance, then stay up all night dancing to a techno beat.

LONGER: ENJOYING NEW YORK CITY TO THE FULL

Spend some days seeing the treasures housed along Museum Mile (see page 18), especially at the Metropolitan Museum of Art (see page 88). Go further afield to explore more city treasures in Brooklyn (see page 132), Queens and the Bronx.

⬥ Having a rest by a peaceful pond in Central Park

Something for nothing

It's very possible to enjoy New York on a budget. For starters, consider a free tour with local volunteers through **Big Apple Greeters** (❶ (212) 669 8159 Ⓦ www.bigapplegreeter.org) or neighbourhood organisations like **The Village Alliance** (❶ (212) 777 2173 Ⓦ www.villagealliance.org). The free **Downtown Connection** bus (Ⓦ www.downtownny.com) travels from Chambers Street around Manhattan's tip to South Street Seaport, making stops in between. Kayak on the Hudson River for free from the **Downtown Boathouse** (❸ Pier 40 at Houston & the Hudson River ❶ (646) 613 0375/0740 Ⓦ www.downtownboathouse.org).

The free **Staten Island Ferry** (❸ Whitehall Terminal, 1 Whitehall St ❶ (718) 815 2628 Ⓦ www.siferry.com) provides a veritable cruise,

⬥ *Lower East Side street market*

CITYPASS

Buy a **CityPass** (ⓦ www.citypass.com) for discounted admission to six sites – the American Museum of Natural History (see page 98), the Metropolitan Museum of Art and the Guggenheim Museum (see page 88), Museum of Modern Art (see page 66), the Empire State Building Observatory (see page 64) and Circle Line Sightseeing Cruises (see page 40). Tickets can be bought online, at visitor centres (see page 152) or at the first attraction you visit, and are valid for nine days.

passing (from a distance) Ellis Island and Lady Liberty (see page 77). Time this trip for a glorious sunset, with postcard views of Manhattan and its bridges.

Brooklyn Brewery has tours every Saturday (ⓐ 79 N 11th St ⓘ (718) 486 7422 ⓒ Tours: 13.00, 14.00, 15.00, 16.00, 17.00 ⓦ www.brooklynbrewery.com ⓘ Minimum age 21). Back in Manhattan, the World Financial Center hosts art exhibits, music and films throughout the year in the lobby-level **Winter Garden** (ⓐ 200 Liberty St).

Gratis salsa and tango lessons can be found on Tuesdays and Fridays respectively at **Chelsea Market** (ⓐ 75 Ninth Ave ⓦ www.chelseamarket.com ⓒ 08.00–17.00). The Museum at **Fashion Institute of Technology (FIT)** is (freely) devoted to fashion (ⓐ Seventh Ave at 27th St ⓘ (212) 217 4558 ⓦ www.fitnyc.edu/museum ⓒ 12.00–20.00 Tues Fri, 10.00–17.00 Sat, closed Sun & Mon).

Learn about the birds and bees for free at **Queens Botanical Garden** (ⓐ 43 Main St ⓘ (718) 886 3800 ⓦ www.queensbotanical.org ⓒ 08.00–16.30 Tues–Sun (Nov–Mar); 08.00–18.00 Tues–Sun (Apr–Oct); closed Mon).

When it rains

If the weather is cold or wet, make an occasion of it by splurging on a restorative high tea at the elegant **Palm Court** in the Plaza Hotel (📍 Fifth Ave at Central Park South 🕐 (212) 759 3000 🕐 14.00–17.00). Or, perhaps, indulge in some star-gazing at **Grand Central Terminal** (see page 47), especially if a bout of inclement weather coincides with one of the twice-weekly free tours. If you're feeling conscientious, you can catch up on your email at the **New York Public Library**, a splendid beaux arts building (📍 Fifth Ave & 42nd St 🕐 (917) 275 6975 🌐 www.nypl.org 🕐 10.00–18.00 Mon, 11.00–19.30 Tues & Wed, 11.00–18.00 Thur–Sat, 13.00–17.00 Sun).

Of course, one thing you can do when it rains is go for a walk in Central Park (see page 12) – take an umbrella and you'll find it's a strangely romantic and peaceful experience. Alternatively, you can ice-skate, indoors, year-round at **Chelsea Piers' Sky Rink** (📍 Pier 61, W 23rd St at Hudson River 🕐 (212) 336 6100 🕐 13.30–17.20 Mon & Fri, 15.00–17.30 Tues & Thur, 13.00–15.50 Sat & Sun, closed Wed ℹ Admission charge). If you don't want to break into a sweat, luxuriate instead at **Elizabeth Arden's Red Door** (📍 691 Fifth Ave 🕐 (212) 546 0398 🕐 08.00–17.00 Mon & Tues, 08.00–21.00 Wed & Thur, 08.00–20.00 Fri, 08.00–19.00 Sat, 09.00–18.00 Sun).

Taking the Gray Line tour (see page 56)? Don't worry, they courteously provide rain ponchos, so you get to stay dry and your style rating goes through the roof. No matter how hydrophobic you are, the rain needn't keep you indoors. You can be sure that opportunistic entrepreneurs will be selling umbrellas at subway exits – to you (and you only), at rock-bottom prices.

⬥ Macy's is famous for its holiday window displays

On arrival

TIME DIFFERENCE

New York follows Eastern Standard Time (EST). During Daylight Saving Time (mid-Mar to early Nov), clocks are put ahead one hour.

ARRIVING

By air

Two major international airports serve New York, and the website ⓦ www.panynj.gov gives detailed airport and transportation information on all New York airports. The largest, **John F Kennedy Airport**, known as **JFK** (ⓐ JFK Expy & S Cargo Rd ① (718) 244 4444 ⓦ www.kennedyairport.com), is 24 km (15 miles) from midtown Manhattan. Each of its nine terminals has currency exchange, ATM and car rental. For public transit, follow signs marked 'Ground Transportation' to exit the airport.

Taxis (① (212) 639 9675 ⓦ www.nyc.gov/taxi) – known as yellow cabs – wait outside the baggage reclaim area, taking 30–60 minutes to Manhattan. Accept rides only from uniformed agents at the taxi stand. Shared vans cost half the price, with door-to-door service, but they make several stops; one good outfit is **SuperShuttle** (① (212) 209 7000 ⓦ www.supershuttle.com).

Buses from **New York Airport Service** (① (718) 875 8200 ⓦ www.nyairportservice.com) take the same amount of time as taxis, departing every 15–30 minutes for about $15 to Grand Central Terminal, Penn Station and Port Authority Bus Terminal. Hotel drop-offs are available as well.

Subway (underground metro) alternatives that avoid congested traffic are far cheaper than going by road, but are tedious, cumbersome and time-consuming. **AirTrain** (① (800) 247 7433

Ⓦ www.mta.info) costs $5 and connects to the subway for an additional $2.25 (it's free for connections between JFK's terminals, parking areas and rental-car facilities).

Newark Liberty Airport (Ⓐ North Ave & Spring St, Elizabeth, NJ Ⓣ (973) 961 6000 Ⓦ www.newarkairport.com) is located in New Jersey, 26 km (16 miles) away from the city, and also services the New York metro area. Taxis to the centre cost between $50 and $70. Buses cost between $15 and $21 and depart from the 'Ground Transportation' area. **Newark Liberty Airport Express** (Ⓣ (877) 863 9275 Ⓦ www.coachusa.com) connects to the Port Authority Bus Terminal and the train stations, as well as to Chinatown and the Wall Street area. **AirTrain** (Ⓣ (888) 397 4636 Ⓦ www.airtrainnewark.com) costs about $15 and connects to Penn Station via the new Rail Link Station. Follow signs marked 'Monorail/AirTrain Link'.

Fiorello LaGuardia Airport (Ⓐ Hangar 7 Center, Third Floor, Flushing Ⓣ (718) 533 3400 Ⓦ www.laguardiaairport.com) services mostly domestic flights, plus Canada and the Caribbean, and it is only 14 km (9 miles) from Manhattan. Metered taxi rides run from $20 to $30 for the 20-minute ride to midtown. Buses and shared van services are similar in cost to JFK (New York Airport Service shuttle between LaGuardia and Manhattan is $12).

Whichever airport you use, remember that traffic can be treacherous; leave early for flights, and avoid illegal 'gypsy' cabs.

By rail
Pennsylvania Station (Ⓐ 33rd St, between 7th & 8th Aves Ⓣ (800) 872 7245) on New York's West Side is home to **Amtrak** trains (Ⓣ (800) 872 7245 Ⓦ www.amtrak.com), which arrive from all over the US. It also serves Long Island and New Jersey. **Grand Central Terminal** (Ⓐ 42nd St at Park Ave Ⓣ (212) 532 4900

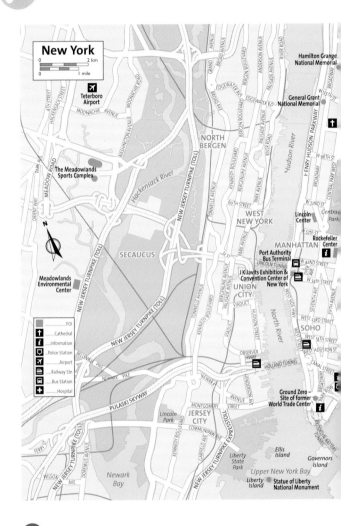

New York

0 _____ 2 km

0 _____ 1 mile

Teterboro Airport

Hamilton Grange National Memorial

General Grant National Memorial

NORTH BERGEN

The Meadowlands Sports Complex

Hudson River

WEST NEW YORK

Lincoln Center

Central Park

Rockefeller Center

MANHATTAN

Port Authority Bus Terminal

J K Javits Exhibition & Convention Center of New York

Meadowlands Environmental Center

SECAUCUS

UNION CITY

North River

SOHO

POI

Cathedral

Information

Police Station

Airport

Railway Stn

Bus Station

Hospital

HOLLAND TUNNEL

Ground Zero – Site of former World Trade Center

PULASKI SKYWAY

JERSEY CITY

Lincoln Park

Newark Bay

Liberty State Park

Ellis Island

Governors Island

Upper New York Bay

Liberty Island

Statue of Liberty National Monument

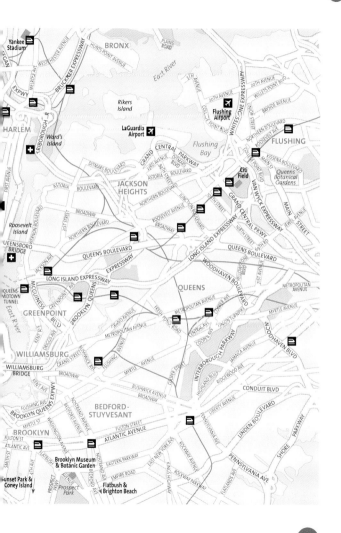

Ⓦ www.grandcentralterminal.com) is across town on the East
Side, and primarily serves commuter destinations in the suburbs.
Both stations have a full complement of tourist amenities as well
as some noted restaurants and are easily reached by taxi, bus
or subway.

By road

The **Port Authority Bus Terminal** at Eighth Avenue between 40th
and 42nd Streets (Ⓣ (212) 564 8484) is a busy place, but it's highly
organised, with connections to nearly everywhere on the North
American continent. Amenities are vast and include a post office,
ATMs, parking and even a bowling alley, **Leisure Time Bowl**
(Ⓐ 625 Eighth Ave Ⓣ (212) 268 6909 Ⓦ www.leisuretimebowl.com
Ⓛ 10.00–24.00 Mon–Wed, 10.00–02.00 Thur, 10.00–03.00 Fri,
11.00–03.00 Sat, 11.00–23.00 Sun).

If you want to drive yourself, be aware that Manhattan is mostly
laid out on a grid pattern (but some areas are still a confusing
jumble of streets). It's right-hand drive in the US, and parking rates
in New York run up to $40 a day. Each weekday morning, most
bridges and tunnels are closed to single inbound drivers for four
hours. Note that it's illegal to drive with a mobile phone in your hand.

The best advice is simply not to drive; instead, do what New
Yorkers do and use public transport. The subway runs underground
and avoids the snarled traffic just above. If driving is a must, reserve
parking through **Icon Parking Systems** (Ⓦ www.weparknewyork.com).

FINDING YOUR FEET

From every approach to the city, travellers get a glimpse of the
great skyscrapers high above Manhattan Island's granite base.
You should get your bearings by taking a brief walk around your

hotel's neighbourhood. You will immediately have a sense of the city's bustling crowds, beautiful buildings and delectable shops.

Stop by New York City's Official Visitor Information Center (see page 152) and make a day's plan or visit the website before your trip so you can hit the ground running.

⬤ Landmarks such as the Empire State Building help you get your bearings

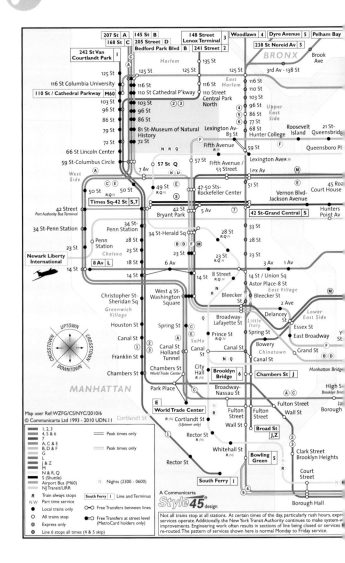

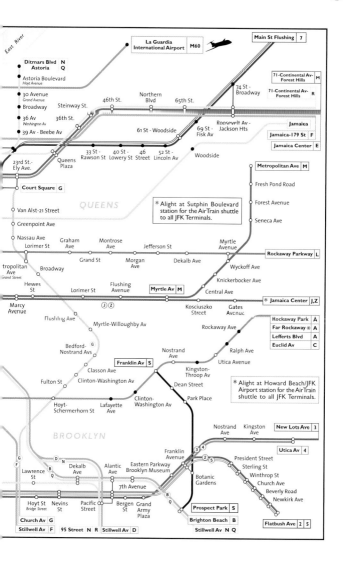

Leave maps tucked away well out of sight and walk with a sense of purpose. The city is safer now than just a few years ago. However, as in most large cities, be aware of your personal belongings on public transport and in crowds and be cautious at night – avoid being alone in unfamiliar dark places or in parks. Look both ways before crossing any street as some are two-way.

ORIENTATION

The island of Manhattan has such a wealth of sights that many visitors don't realise it is only one of five boroughs that belong to New York City. In fact, it is the smallest in size – 21 km (13 miles) long and only 3.7 km (2^1/$_3$ miles) wide – but is packed with attractions. Brooklyn and the other boroughs, as well as New Jersey, are linked to Manhattan by many bridges, tunnels and ferries.

Fifth Avenue is the dividing line between East and West for street addresses. Building numbers increase with distance away from Fifth Avenue, about a hundred per block. There are a dozen north/south major Avenues, numbered First Avenue to Twelfth Avenue (a few have names such as Lexington, Park, Madison, Broadway). Avenue of the Americas is the formal name for what everyone calls Sixth Avenue. Approximately twelve north–south blocks equal 1 km (20 blocks to a mile). Most streets are one-way; traffic travels in both directions on some wide streets including 14th, 23rd, 34th, 42nd, 57th, 72nd and 86th. Conveniently, most subway stations are located on these same streets; subway lines are INT, BMT and IRT.

From Greenwich Village northwards, the city is primarily a grid, so it is nearly impossible to get lost. In the subway system (or even if you are walking), Downtown and Uptown refer to the direction in which you are going – for example, if you are travelling from 59th Street to 34th Street, you would be going Downtown. Below

14th Street and throughout the lower part of Manhattan, the grid-like city pattern falls away and things can get messy.

GETTING AROUND

Most people get around the city by bus or subway at $2.25 per ride, regardless of distance. You must purchase a Metropolitan Transit Authority (MTA) **MetroCard** (W www.mta.info/metrocard) to ride

⬤ Look out for impressive mural art

subways or buses. MetroCard vending machines are located in subway stations and accept cash and credit or debit cards. Unlimited-ride MetroCards permit hop-on, hop-off travel. Subway rides are fast; buses are handy for short trips and good for the sightseeing, but they can be slow in traffic. The MetroCard includes some museum discounts, too.

During a short stay, it's wise to plan carefully how to navigate through the city, in order to see as much as possible. The **Metropolitan Transit Authority (MTA) Trip Planner** (Ⓦ www.tripplanner.mta.info) is a useful tool for figuring out the best way to get from Point A to Point B. While you're at New York City's Official Visitor Information Center (see page 152), buy a CityPass (see page 43) or MetroCard. Book a red double-decker London-style **Gray Line** bus tour (Ⓐ 777 Eighth Ave Ⓣ (800) 669 0051 Ⓦ www.newyorksightseeing.com); there are 50 stops in Manhattan and Brooklyn. A 48-hour ticket costs about $50 and permits hop-on, hop-off travel on three tour loops, from 08.00 to 18.00. Check the website as there may be online discounts.

Yellow metered taxis (also called 'cabs') are everywhere and can be hailed from the street. Available taxis travel with a rooftop number lit, but they won't stop for customers if the sign's 'Off Duty' portion is lit.

CAR HIRE

Car hire can be arranged at the airport, and national rental companies such as **Avis** (Ⓣ (800) 331 1212 Ⓦ www.avis.com) have several locations in the city. Rates tend to be high in the New York area.

Ⓞ *Gothic-style St Patrick's Cathedral*

THE CITY OF
New York

Midtown Manhattan

No one questions that midtown Manhattan is the epitome of New York, and its heart is fervently beating here, among the skyscrapers and mass of people. Photographs of the New York skyline are iconic, but midtown Manhattan comes to mind when someone says 'New York' or simply 'The City'. Skyscrapers stand tall like stalks of asparagus in a corded bunch, many of the top sightseeing attractions are within walking distance of each other; and there is a huge collection of grand hotels and cosmopolitan shops. Despite cold weather, Christmas in New York warms the spirit, and is a wonderful time to visit. Lights twinkle in all the plazas, roasted chestnuts are sold on street corners, and shop windows are dressed up like scenes from fairy tales.

Midtown runs along Fifth Avenue from 34th to 59th Streets, stretching east to the East River and west to the Hudson River. Numbered streets and avenues make getting around the area very easy. Everything is on the move here – people, cabs, trucks, bikes and buses. However, traffic gets completely snarled from Central Park all the way down to the Empire State Building. Midtown gives a total immersion into urban living. Stop to see famous statues, such as Atlas holding an Art Deco world, or watch a mime performer on any corner, with cars honking horns as the background music.

SIGHTS & ATTRACTIONS

Chrysler Building

Resembling a car topped with hubcap-style gargoyles, the Art Deco building is a distinctive city landmark. An impressive mural in the

lobby screams Fred Astaire and Ginger Rogers. 405 Lexington Ave (Lobby hours) 08.00–18.00 Mon–Fri, closed Sat & Sun Subway: 4, 5, 6, 7 to Grand Central Terminal

Grand Army Plaza

The postcard scene of horse-drawn carriages in this beautiful plaza with its Pulitzer Fountain and a statue of Pomona, the Roman goddess of abundance, is a focal point of the midtown area. Whether heading into the park or on your way down Fifth Avenue, this is a wide-open space to stop and catch your breath, and to do a little people-watching. 59th St & Fifth Ave Subway: N, R, 4, 5, 6 to 59th St; F to 57th St

Great White Way (Broadway) & Times Square

Two huge avenues converge to make the triangle known as Times Square. As dusk settles in, the lights on theatre marquees and giant billboards light up with an intoxicating brilliance, giving this stretch of Broadway its nickname. Hundreds of thousands of revellers gather here on New Year's Eve to see the ball drop, while another billion people watch on television. A collection of theatres lines the side streets west of Times Square; like almost everything else, theatre inched its way uptown from the Bowery to 42nd Street. From Vaudeville and the Ziegfeld Follies, through great stars like the Marx Brothers, to the ultimate of sleaze in the 1970s and 1980s, the Great White Way is now in a dazzling, new era. Old theatres have been restored, and new ones share the street with MTV and Toys 'Я' Us. Take a walk, or see a show – in the triangle where the neon never dims. 1 Times Sq www.timessquare.com Subway: N, Q, R, S, 1, 2, 3, 7 to Times Sq–42nd St

⬥ The Chrysler Building, built in the Art Deco style

Rockefeller Center

A sloping path through the Channel Gardens leads to Rockefeller Center's sunken plaza, surrounded by international flags and the rink where skaters dance across the ice. The gardens are decorated each season, especially at Christmas when an enormous Norway Spruce Christmas tree is lit. The Center is an outdoor Art Deco museum, with its beautiful 1930s buildings and many sculptures, including the prominent *Prometheus* that presides over the rink. More than 20 buildings are linked by an underground concourse with myriad shops and eateries. You can grab a lunch-to-go and picnic near the

⬥ *Prometheus looks over the courtyard of the Rockefeller Center*

gardens, or settle in at the Rock Center Café to watch the skaters and have a leisurely meal. 🅐 Rockefeller Center 🅣 (212) 332 6868 🅦 www.rockefellercenter.com 🅛 08.30–17.30 Mon–Sat, 09.30–16.30 Sun 🅢 Subway: F, B, D to Rockefeller Center; 6 to E 51st St–Lexington Ave; 1 to 50th St–Broadway; N, R to 49th St

St Patrick's Cathedral

The lofty spires of the decorated Gothic-style Catholic cathedral pierce the air over Fifth Avenue. Walk inside to see its impressive size, beautiful stained-glass windows and a giant organ. The cathedral holds 2,200 people and is the seat of the Archdiocese of New York. 🅐 51st St & Fifth Ave 🅣 (212) 753 2261 🅦 www.saintpatrickscathedral.org 🅛 06.30–20.45 🅢 Subway: B, D, F, M to 47th–50th Sts

Top of the Rock™

From the observation deck, designed with an ocean-liner theme, visitors enjoy 70th-floor views and the sparkling lights of the city and beyond. Tickets must be reserved in advance, which helps avoid queues. 🅐 30 Rockefeller Plaza 🅣 (212) 698 2000 🅦 www.topoftherocknyc.com 🅛 08.00–24.00 🅢 Subway: B, D, F, M to 47th–50th Sts–Rockefeller Center; N, R to 49th St–Seventh Ave; E to 53rd St–Fifth Ave; 6 to E 51st St–Lexington Ave; 1 to 50th St–Broadway

United Nations

The flags of all member nations of the UN wave outside this large complex devoted to worldwide peace and security. Tours include a visit to the Security Council, the domed General Assembly Hall, and artworks throughout. 🅐 46th St & First Ave 🅣 (212) 963 8687 🅦 www.un.org 🅛 09.45–16.45 Mon–Fri, closed Sat & Sun 🅢 Subway: 4, 5, 6, 7 to 42nd St–Grand Central Station

EMPIRE STATE BUILDING

The Art Deco building's size, at 102 floors and 381 m (1,250 ft) high, made it the tallest skyscraper in the world when it was built in 1931. It held that record for over 40 years, until the World Trade Center was finished. Thrilling panoramic views are seen from the observation tower, including many city landmarks. When it's windy, you can feel the building sway. Queues can be long so purchase tickets online – an Express Pass moves you to the front of the line, or buy a CityPass in advance. 🄰 350 Fifth Ave 🄣 (212) 736 3100 🄦 www.esbnyc.com 🄲 08.00–02.00 🄝 Subway: A, C, E, 1, 2, 3 to 34th St–Penn Station; B, D, F, N, Q, R to 34th St–Herald Sq

CULTURE

Midtown has its share of museums, but it's the MoMA (Museum of Modern Art, see page 66) that everyone comes to see. Smaller museums of note are the **American Folk Art Museum** (🄰 45 W 53rd St 🄣 (212) 265 1040 🄦 www.folkartmuseum.org 🄲 10.30–17.30 Tues–Thur, Sat & Sun, 10.30–19.30 Fri, closed Mon) and the **International Center of Photography** (🄰 1133 Ave of the Americas 🄣 (212) 857 0000 🄦 www.icp.org 🄲 10.00–18.00 Tues–Thur, Sat & Sun, 10.00–20.00 Fri, closed Mon).

Carnegie Hall

There's nothing quite like being in this acoustically perfect hall for a big concert, packed 2,800 strong with an enthusiastic crowd. The programme includes many music genres from hot jazz and soloists

🔺 The iconic Empire State Building and star-spangled banner

to classical orchestras. ⓐ 154 W 57th St ⓘ Box office: (212) 247 7800;
Tour hotline: (212) 903 9765 ⓦ www.carnegiehall.org ⓒ Tours: 11.30,
12.30, 14.00 & 15.00 Mon–Fri, 11.30 & 12.30 Sat, 12.30 Sun ⓝ Subway:
A, B, C, D, 1 to Columbus Circle; E, N, Q, R to 57th St–Seventh Ave
ⓘ Tour times can vary, so call ahead

The Morgan Library & Museum

This delightful small museum, set in a quiet neighbourhood, houses
rare manuscripts and priceless works by authors Mark Twain and
Lewis Carroll among many others. ⓐ 225 Madison Ave ⓘ (212) 685 0008
ⓦ www.morganlibrary.org ⓒ 10.30–17.00 Tues–Thur, 10.30–21.00 Fri,
10.00–18.00 Sat, 11.00–18.00 Sun, closed Mon ⓝ Bus: M2, M3, M4,
Q32 to 36th St; Subway: 6 to 33rd St; 4, 5, 7 to Grand Central Station;
B, D, F, Q to 42nd St ⓘ Admission charge (except Fri)

Museum of Modern Art (MoMA)

A walk through the MoMA is like taking a walk through the
illustrated history of 20th-century art. Here you can gaze at real-life
originals of images that have been seen over and over again in
books and magazines. Room after room is filled with great paintings
such as Cézanne's *The Bather* and Van Gogh's *The Starry Night*. Also
represented are earthy Gauguin paintings, Cubist-era paintings by
Pablo Picasso and Monet's *Water Lilies*. There's the surrealism of Dalí,
and colour-splashed canvasses by Jackson Pollock and Mark Rothko.
The museum houses a Sculpture Garden and there's also a huge
collection of photography. ⓐ 11 W 53rd St ⓘ (212) 708 9400
ⓦ www.moma.org ⓒ 10.30–17.30 Sat–Mon, Wed & Thur,
10.30–20.00 Fri, closed Tues ⓝ Subway: E, M to 53rd St–Fifth Ave;
B, D, F to 47th–50th Sts–Rockefeller Center
ⓘ Admission charge

RETAIL THERAPY

Fifth Avenue is a long shopping centre, and creatively designed shop windows are its trademark. You'll stroll by great designer shops like **Gucci** (ⓐ 725 Fifth Ave ⓣ (212) 826 2600), chic department stores like **Bergdorf Goodman** (ⓐ 754 Fifth Ave ⓣ (212) 753 7300 ⓦ www.bergdorfgoodman.com), and – across the street – **Louis Vuitton** (ⓐ 1 East 57th St ⓣ (212) 758 8877 ⓦ www.louisvuitton.com). Jewellers who sell to celebrities and billionaires are here, too – **Bulgari** (ⓐ 730 Fifth Ave ⓣ (212) 315 9000) and the **House of Harry Winston** (ⓐ 718 Fifth Ave ⓣ (212) 245 2000 ⓦ www.harrywinston.com), for example.

Rockefeller Center (see page 62) alone is filled with shops from **Banana Republic** (ⓐ 626 Fifth Ave ⓣ (212) 974 2350) to **Barnes and Noble** (ⓐ 555 Fifth Ave ⓣ (212) 697 3048). You can also repair a watch there, or get your shoes shined. Many shops are open on Sundays. If you need a brief respite, slip into Paley's Vest Pocket Park on E 53rd Street between Fifth and Madison Avenues.

Anthropologie Ladies, get thee to Anthropologie, where you'll find fresh, fun(ctional), fun(ky) feminine clothing and delightful accessories. Home furnishings have a French, shabby-chic vibe. Great for gifts. Several locations in the city. ⓐ 50 Rockefeller Center ⓣ (212) 246 0386 ⓦ www.anthropologie.com ⓛ 10.00–20.00 Mon–Sat, 11.00–19.00 Sun ⓝ Subway: B, D, F, M to 47th–50th Sts; N, R to 49th St

Apple Store Part sculpture and pure Mac cool, the 9.75 m (32 ft) cubic glass entrance turns heads. Shop the subterranean shelves for all the latest and greatest from this computer giant. ⓐ 767 Fifth Ave ⓣ (212) 336 1440 ⓛ 24 hours ⓝ Subway: N, R to 59th St– Fifth Ave

The Diamond District A single street is devoted to jewellery and diamonds, where you can probably find a nice rock at wholesale prices – if buying, be sure to compare. All along W 47th Street, west of Fifth Avenue, Hasidic dealers duck and dive in close quarters, among the 2,600 shops. ● (212) 302 5739 ⓦ www.diamonddistrict.org ● Most shops 09.30–17.30 Mon–Fri, closed Sat & Sun ⓝ Subway: see Rockefeller Center (page 62)

FAO Schwarz Spend some time shopping in this engaging emporium of toys and you'll feel like a child again. Hug soft, lush teddy bears to your heart, hop out a tune on the larger-than-life Dance-On-Piano and don't leave without stopping at FAO Schweetz for a towering milkshake or frosty ice-cream float. ⓐ 767 Fifth Ave ● (212) 644 9400 ⓦ www.fao.com ● 10.00–19.00 Mon–Thur, 10.00–20.00 Fri & Sat, 11.00–18.00 Sun ⓝ Subway: N, R to 59th St–Fifth Ave; 4, 5, 6 to 59th St–Lexington Ave

Tiffany & Co. Taking home anything wrapped in the trademark blue box and tied with a white satin ribbon is symbolic of buying elegance. You can find little treasures at Tiffany's for under $100. ⓐ 727 Fifth Ave ● (212) 755 8000 ⓦ www.tiffany.com ● 10.00–19.00 Mon–Sat, 12.00–18.00 Sun ⓝ Subway: N, R to 59th St–Fifth Ave; 4, 5, 6 to 59th St–Lexington Ave

TAKING A BREAK

With all the hustle and bustle, you'll need a break. Slip over to the East River and ride the tram to **Roosevelt Island** (Tram entrance ⓐ 59th St & Second Ave ● (212) 832 4555 ⓦ www.rioc.com ● 06.00–02.00 Sun–Thur, 06.00–03.00 Fri & Sat, every

🔺 *World-famous Tiffany & Co. on Fifth Avenue*

15 minutes), or stroll through the elegant Sutton Place neighbourhood. If you're now used to the crowds, picnic in Rockefeller Center (see page 62) or **Bryant Park**. ❷ Between 40th and 42nd Sts Ⓝ Subway: B, D, F, M to 42nd St–Bryant Park. Alternatively, head west to Ninth Avenue for a bevy of international lunch options.

Ben & Jerry's £ ❶ Get a sugar boost with scrumptious Vermont ice cream. ❷ 30 Rockefeller Center ❶ (212) 218 7843 Ⓦ www.benjerry.com ❶ 10.00–20.00 Mon–Fri, 11.00–20.00 Sat, 11.00–18.00 Sun Ⓝ Subway: F, B, D to Rockefeller Center; 6 to 51st St–Lexington Ave; 1 to 50th St–Broadway; N, R to 49th St

Dean & Deluca £ ❷ Another picnic ingredients spot; get some delicacies to munch on here. ❷ 9 Rockefeller Plaza ❶ (212) 664 1363 Ⓦ www.deananddeluca.com ❶ 07.00–20.00 Ⓝ Subway: F, B, D to Rockefeller Center; 6 to 51st St–Lexington Ave; 1 to 50th St–Broadway; N, R to 49th St

Island Burgers 'N' Shakes £ ❸ Choose from 65 creative varieties of burgers and chicken sandwiches, such as the 'Route 66' with avocado, Swiss cheese and bacon on dark rye, or the 'Bangkok' with Thai chilli, curry and peanut sauce. ❷ 766 Ninth Ave ❶ (212) 307 7934 Ⓦ www.islandburgersny.com ❶ 12.00–22.30 Mon–Thur, Sat & Sun, 12.00–23.00 Fri Ⓝ Subway: C, E to 50th St

Carnegie Deli ££ ❹ This quintessential New York Jewish deli is seen in Woody Allen's film, *Broadway Danny Rose*. It's famous for gigantic heart-attack sandwiches filled with corned beef, pastrami brisket and chopped liver. ❷ 854 Seventh Ave ❶ (800) 334 5606

Ⓦ www.carnegiedeli.com Ⓛ 06.30–04.00 Ⓝ Subway: B, D, E to Seventh Ave; N, R to 57th St

Oyster Bar & Restaurant ££ ➎ Under an impressive curved and tiled ceiling and purportedly below sea level, gulp down some super-fresh Long Island Blue Points in the Oyster Bar. Before you leave, take time to marvel at the restored cathedral ceiling – a night sky with stars and constellations. Ⓐ Grand Central Station Ⓣ (212) 490 6650 Ⓦ www.oysterbarny.com Ⓛ 11.30–21.30 Mon–Fri, 12.00–21.30 Sat, closed Sun Ⓝ Subway: S, 4, 5, 6, 7 to 42nd St–Grand Central Station

Rock Center Café ££ ➏ Watch the ice-skating while lunching in style. Ⓐ 20 W 50th St Ⓣ (212) 332 7620 Ⓦ www.rapatina.com Ⓛ 07.30–10.30, 11.30–15.00, 17.00–22.00 Mon–Fri, 11.00–15.00, 16.00–22.00 Sat, 10.00–15.00, 16.00–21.00 Sun Ⓝ Subway: see Rockefeller Center (page 62)

Algonquin Hotel ££–£££ ➐ Stop for a drink and soak up the literary atmosphere of this historic hotel. Swing by later for an evening of cabaret in the Oak Room. Ⓐ 59 W 44th St Ⓣ (212) 840 6800 Ⓦ www.algonquinhotel.com Ⓛ (The Blue Bar) 11.30–01.30 Ⓝ Subway: B, D, F, M to 42nd St

AFTER DARK

If you want to see real stars, take a ride to the top of the Marriott Marquis in Times Square to **The View** (Ⓐ 1535 Broadway Ⓣ (212) 704 8900), New York's only revolving rooftop restaurant. Some of the city's best restaurants are in midtown, but prices tend to be skyscraper-high.

RESTAURANTS

Toloache ££ In the heart of the theatre district, this Mexican eatery dishes out modern translations of traditional fare and boasts 100 varieties of tequila. Décor details like imported tiles and tin lanterns transport you to Mexico City. ⓐ 251 W 50th St ⓣ (212) 581 1818 ⓦ www.toloachenyc.com ⓛ 11.30–15.00 daily, 17.00–23.00 Sun–Thur, 17.00–23.30 Fri & Sat ⓝ Subway: A, C, E to 49th St

Aquavit £££ Three-course *prix fixe* dinners and table-tasting menus of contemporary Scandinavian cuisine are available in the main dining room of this stylish restaurant. You'll find Swedish meatballs and gravadlax, as well as hot-smoked sautéed salmon and grilled flank of venison. Save room for the Sunday all-you-can-eat brunch. ⓐ 65 E 55th St ⓣ (212) 307 7311 ⓦ www.aquavit.org ⓛ Brunch: 11.30–15.00 Sat & Sun, Lunch: 11.30–15.00 Mon–Fri, Dinner: 15.00–22.00 Sun & Mon, 15.00–23.00 Tues–Thur, 15.00–24.00 Fri & Sat ⓝ Subway: 6 to 51st St; E, M to Lexington Ave–53rd St

Bar Americain £££ Celebrity chef Bobby Flay holds court at this American brasserie that's always crowded, especially for brunch on the weekends. ⓐ 152 W 52nd St ⓣ (212) 265 9700 ⓦ www.baramericain.com ⓛ 11.45–14.30 & 17.00–22.00 Mon–Fri, 11.30–14.30 & 17.00–00.30 Sat & Sun ⓝ Subway: N, R to 49th St; Q to 57th St

Le Bernardin £££ Said to be one of New York's best restaurants. Seafood is cooked to perfection, topped with delicacies like sea urchin or truffles. There are some tasting menus that help bring down the expense of trying out a restaurant of this calibre.

ⓐ 155 W 51st St ⓣ (212) 554 1515 ⓦ www.le-bernardin.com
ⓛ 12.00–14.30 Mon–Fri, 17.30–22.30 Mon–Thur, 17.30–23.00 Fri & Sat,
closed Sun ⓝ Subway: B, D, F, M to 47th–50th Sts–Rockefeller Center

CINEMAS & THEATRES

Radio City Music Hall Since its opening, the Rockettes have thrilled
audiences with their leggy precision and high-kick dance. They
perform the *Christmas Spectacular* and *Easter Show*. The Art Deco
interior is worth the ticket price. ⓐ 1260 Sixth Ave ⓛ Stage Door
Tours: 11.30–18.00 Mon–Sat ⓣ (212) 307 7171 ⓦ www.radiocity.com
ⓝ Subway: see Rockefeller Center (page 62)

BARS & CLUBS

Birdland Catch the best names in jazz at the latest incarnation
of this legendary club. ⓐ 315 W 44th St ⓣ (212) 581 3080
ⓦ www.birdlandjazz.com ⓛ Show times are 20.30 and 23.00
unless otherwise stated ⓝ Subway: A, C, E to 42nd St
ⓘ Admission charge

P J Clarke's This tenacious little saloon has been around since the
mid-1800s. After a renovation and a few menu additions, the juicy
cheeseburgers are still its prize dish. Icons Frank Sinatra and
Nat King Cole once enjoyed the casual atmosphere. ⓐ 915 Third Ave
ⓣ (212) 317 1616 ⓦ www.pjclarkes.com ⓛ 11.30–04.00 ⓝ Subway: E,
M to Lexington Ave; F, N, R, 4, 5, 6 to 59th St; 6 to 51st St

Pacha You can dance the night away in this four-storey *über*club
along the Hudson River. ⓐ 618 W 46th St ⓣ (212) 209 7500
ⓦ www.pachanyc.com ⓛ 10.00–06.00 Fri & Sat, closed Sun–Thur
ⓝ Subway: A, C, E to 42nd St

Financial District & Chinatown

A belt of green wraps around the thumb-tip of Manhattan, full of small idyllic picnic spots with views stretching from the harbour to the Statue of Liberty (see page 77). It's hardly a harbinger of the frenetic activity around Wall Street, just a few blocks north. Long ago, Downtown was the city's heart and soul and, ever so briefly, the country's capital. At that point, Downtown ended abruptly at City Hall, with only farmland beyond. City Hall's northern façade was even left unfinished as it was presumed that no one would see it, and no one imagined the future northward exodus into the farmland areas.

Nearly every corner of this area took part in the city's history, so to get a real feel for the place it's best to walk around. The free Downtown Connection bus (see page 42) helps when feet get tired. Most of New York's oldest buildings are here – **Trinity Church** (🚇 74 Trinity Place ☎ (212) 602 0800) and the graveyard where Alexander Hamilton rests, the **Woolworth Building**'s gilded hall (🚇 233 Broadway) and Broadway's so-called Canyon of Heroes area, where ticker-tape parades celebrate the brave. With the continued excavation of the World Trade Center site, demolition of surrounding damaged buildings, construction of the Freedom Tower and the National September 11 Museum and Memorial, as well as creation of the Fulton Street Transit Center and Santiago Calatrava-design World Trade Center Transportation Hub/ PATH terminal, Lower Manhattan is in the midst of transformation.

SIGHTS & ATTRACTIONS

African Burial Ground National Monument

The remains of 419 Africans were discovered in 1991 during pre-construction works on the site of a planned federal building. Now

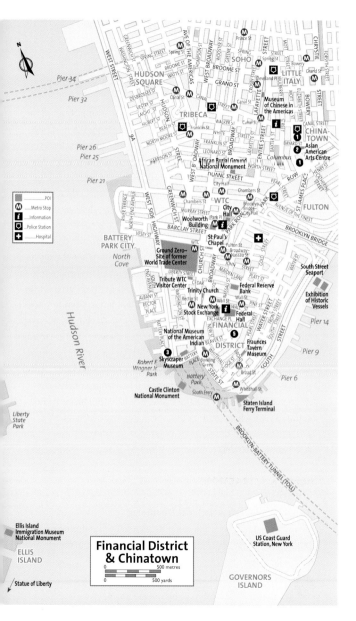

a permanent memorial to 20,000 colonial-era enslaved Africans stands here. Interpretive Center adjacent to the site at 290 Broadway (burial ground on Duane St) (212) 637 2019 www.africanburialground.gov 09.00–17.00 Tues–Sat, closed Sun & Mon Subway: N, Q, R to Canal St; J, Z to Chambers St; 4, 5, 6 to Brooklyn Bridge–City Hall

Battery Park

Among several memorials and statues is *The Sphere*, a remnant of the grand sculpture salvaged from the WTC Plaza. **Castle Clinton National Monument**, the fort from which no one ever fired a shot, underwent various incarnations as a restaurant, then an opera venue, later a gateway for immigrants and an aquarium. The fort is open for tours. Bowling Green & State St www.nps.gov/cacl 08.00–17.00 Subway: R to Whitehall St; 1 to South Ferry; 4, 5 to Bowling Green

Federal Reserve Bank

Billions of dollars' worth of glittering gold bullion are stored 15 m (50 ft) below sea level in the bank vaults of this magnificent neo-Renaissance building. To see the stash by guided tour (every half-hour, on the hour), advance reservations are required at least a week before; call first for availability or email requests to frbnytours@ny.frb.org. 33 Liberty St (212) 720 6130 www.newyorkfed.org 09.30–11.30, 13.30–15.30 Mon–Fri, closed Sat & Sun Subway: 2, 3, 4, 5 to Wall St

St Paul's Chapel

The oldest church in Manhattan, St Paul's is where George Washington prayed under the Waterford glass chandeliers during his first presidential term. Located directly across from the World Trade Center, it quickly became the centre of an enormous volunteer relief effort after the 11 September 2001 attacks. See the exhibit *Unwavering Spirit: Hope & Healing at Ground Zero.* ⓐ 209 Broadway ⓣ (212) 233 4164 ⓦ www.trinitywallstreet.org ⓛ 10.00–18.00 Mon–Sat, 07.00–15.00 Sun ⓜ Subway: E to Chambers Street; R to Cortlandt St; A, 1, 4, 5, 9 to Fulton St–Broadway–Nassau St; 6 to Brooklyn Bridge–City Hall

South Street Seaport
The four-mast *Peking* is just one of the barques alongside the piers in South Street Seaport – an 11-square-block historic district. This complex is full of shops and cafés and has a fish market. ⓐ 19 Fulton St ⓣ (212) SEA PORT ⓦ www.southstseaport.org ⓛ 10.00–21.00 Mon–Sat, 11.00–20.00 Sun ⓜ Subway: A, C to Broadway–Nassau St; J, Z, 2, 3, 4, 5 to Fulton St

Statue of Liberty/Ellis Island Immigration Museum National Monument
The iconic statue, created by sculptor Frédéric Auguste Bartholdi, is a gift from the people of France, honouring the 100-year anniversary of America's independence. It sits on Bedloe Island in New York Harbor, its base graced with the poem by Emma Lazarus *The New Colossus* – 'Give me your tired, your poor, your huddled masses yearning to breathe free...'

From 1892 to 1924, more than 22 million people came through Ellis Island and the Port of New York. The Ellis Island Immigrant Museum provides a fascinating look at the immigration process of the time through photos, artefacts and poignant personal interviews. ⓐ New York Harbor (reached by ferry) ⓣ (212) 363 3200 ⓦ www.nps.gov/stli; Statue Cruises ferry ⓣ (877) 523 9849 ⓦ www.statuecruises.com ⓜ Ferry runs every 30 minutes 09.00–15.30

⬤ *New York's most famous landmark, the Statue of Liberty*

(some seasonal variation); Subway: R to Whitehall St; 1 to South Ferry; 4, 5 to Bowling Green, then take the Statue of Liberty Ferry from the southern part of Battery Park ❶ Backpacks, large bags and pushchairs are not permitted. Admission charge

Tribute WTC Visitor Center

Developed by the September 11th Families' Association as a way for the September 11 community to connect with each other and provide visitors to the World Trade Center site with a person-to-person history of the events of that day, the Center houses five galleries and runs

walking tours of the area conducted by survivors, rescuers, lower Manhattan residents and family members of victims. This is an interim location until completion of the official National September 11th Memorial and Museum, scheduled for September 11, 2012.
🅐 120 Liberty St 🆃 (866) 737 1184 🆆 www.tributewtc.org
🕒 10.00–18.00 Mon, Wed–Sat, 12.00–18.00 Tues, 12.00–17.00 Sun
🄽 Subway: E to World Trade Center; J, Z to Broad St;
1, R to Rector St; 4, 5 to Wall St ❗ Admission charge

Wall Street

Since the attacks of 9/11, Wall Street has been a pedestrian right of way, which suits this narrow street where George Washington was inaugurated as America's first president in 1789. The spot is marked by his statue in front of Federal Hall National Monument. The current building was first a Customs House, then a treasury vault. The **New York Stock Exchange** is dressed in tall Corinthian columns. In pre-9/11 days, one could watch a flurry of activity on the trading floor, where $5 trillion is traded each year. Unfortunately, the Visitor's Gallery is now closed. Federal Hall 🅐 26 Wall St 🆃 (212) 825 6990
🆆 www.nps.gov/feha 🕒 09.00–17.00 Mon–Fri, closed Sat & Sun;
New York Stock Exchange 🅐 20 Broad St 🆆 www.nyse.com
🄽 Subway: 4, 5 to Wall St; J, Z to Broad St

CULTURE

Asian American Arts Centre

Find contemporary art by Asian American artists, as well as performances and folk-art exhibitions. 🅐 111 Norfolk St
🆃 (212) 233 2154 🆆 www.artspiral.org 🕒 12.30–18.30 Tues–Fri, closed Sat–Mon 🄽 Subway: J, N, R, Q, Z, 6 to Canal St

CHINATOWN

Mott Street is home to an enclave of Chinese immigrants. If you happen to visit at the right time of year, you'll enjoy a two-week, colourful festival celebrating Chinese New Year. Cymbals announce multicoloured fabric-covered lion dancers. They wend their way through crowded streets with huge, bobbing, dragon-like heads while costumed men dance in tempo to drums and gongs. Firecrackers blast loudly to scare away evil beasts, and thousands throng the tiny streets to join the parade and festivity.

Chinatown itself is a maze of cobblestone streets filled with Chinese character signs, red pagoda-style storefronts and kitschy shops. Bargain-hunters haggle over Canal Street designer knock-offs, while on Mott Street savvy New Yorkers seek out herbal medicines, exotic vegetables and fresh fish. Crowded restaurants dish up every imaginable Chinese recipe. The total bill is likely to be less than the tax paid in Uptown eateries. ⓐ Mott St & Canal St ⓦ www.explorechinatown.com ⓝ Subway: J, M, N, Q, R, Z, 6 to Canal St; B, D to Grand St; F to E Broadway

Fraunces Tavern Museum

The Tavern, as the oldest building in Manhattan, recalls popular tales from colonial times. The restaurant serves continental fare, but its history is the big attraction. George Washington bade farewell to his officers here in 1783, at a victory banquet in the Long Room, after a grisly revolutionary war. The museum not only has a lock of Washington's hair, but it also has one of his false teeth – a gnasher-nal treasure.

🔺 *New Year celebrations in Chinatown*

ⓐ 54 Pearl St ☏ (212) 425 1778 🌐 www.frauncestavernmuseum.org
🕐 12.00–17.00 Mon–Sat, closed Sun Ⓜ Subway: J, Z to Broad St;
4, 5 to Bowling Green ❶ Admission charge

National Museum of the American Indian

The George Gustav Heye Center at Alexander Hamilton US Custom House is certainly a long title, and it befits such a formidable place. The marble-and-granite beaux arts building itself is remarkable, with its 44 columns topped with the head of Mercury, and a dozen elegant statues above. Carvings, masks, pottery, Navajo weavings, Mayan carved jade and Andean gold are just part of the rich collection brought to this new museum from the Smithsonian Institution. ⓐ 1 Bowling Green ☏ (212) 514 3700 🌐 www.nmai.si.edu 🕐 10.00–17.00 Mon–Wed & Fri–Sun, 10.00–20.00 Thur Ⓜ Subway: R to Whitehall St; 1 to South Ferry; 4, 5 to Bowling Green

Skyscraper Museum

Situated somewhat ironically on the ground floor, sharing a building with the Ritz-Carlton Battery Park (see page 83), this museum delves into the history, design, technology, business and future of this city's architectural hallmark. ⓐ 39 Battery Pl ⓣ (212) 968 1961 ⓦ www.skyscraper.org ⓛ 12.00–18.00 Wed–Sun, closed Mon & Tues ⓝ Subway: 4, 5 to Bowling Green ⓘ Admission charge

TAKING A BREAK

Chinatown Ice Cream Factory £ ❶ Chinese flavours are the speciality at this family-run ice-cream factory. How about an icy Wasabi on a hot day? ⓐ 65 Bayard St ⓣ (212) 608 4170 ⓦ www.chinatownicecreamfactory.com ⓛ 11.00–22.00 ⓝ Subway: J, N, Q, R, Z, 6 to Canal St

⬤ *Baked Alaska is a delicious marvel born at Delmonico's*

New Green Bo £ ❷ While not earning many marks for décor, the restaurant receives praise for its tasty, inexpensive Shanghai-style fare. Grab dessert across the street at the Chinatown Ice Cream Factory. ❸ 66 Bayard St ❶ (212) 625 2359 ❶ 11.00–23.00 ❶ Subway: J, N, Q, R, Z, 6 to Canal St

Rise Bar £ ❶ Go to lofty heights and have a drink at the Rise Bar on the 14th Floor of the Ritz-Carlton for sweeping harbour views, including the Statue of Liberty. ❸ 2 West St ❶ (212) 344 0800 ❶ www.ritzcarlton.com ❶ 16.00–24.00 Sun–Thur, 16.00–02.00 Fri & Sat ❶ Subway: 4, 5 to Bowling Green

AFTER DARK

RESTAURANTS

Wo Hop £ ❹ This downstairs dining room (another Wo Hop exists at street level two doors down) isn't glamorous but the Cantonese food is good, service is friendly, portions are huge and it's almost always open. ❸ 17 Mott St ❶ (212) 962 8617 ❶ 24 hours ❶ Subway: J, N, Q, R, Z to Canal St

Delmonico's ££–£££ ❺ Opened in 1827, this was the first restaurant in the US. For two decades in the mid-1800s, Charles Renhofer, considered in his day to be America's greatest chef, invented trademark dishes for the restaurant that are still on the menu: Lobster Newburg, Baked Alaska and Steak Delmonico. ❸ 56 Beaver St ❶ (212) 509 1144 ❶ www.delmonicosny.com ❶ 11.30–22.00 Mon–Fri, 17.00–22.00 Sat, closed Sun ❶ Subway: 4, 5 to Wall St; J, Z to Broad St

Upper East Side

New York's oil barons and steel magnates spared no expense when building their palatial pads on Fifth Avenue opposite Central Park. The whole Upper East Side has a genteel village ambience with its tree-lined side streets and lovely old brownstone buildings. Central Park breathes fresh air on to the avenue where Jackie O' once dodged paparazzi. The northern part of the Upper East Side, known as Yorkville, was once an enclave of Germans and Hungarians, but few vestiges of those days have lingered. Forget the subway: walk or take a bus to sightsee along this beautiful stretch of the island.

SIGHTS & ATTRACTIONS

Central Park

Not enough can be said about this huge emerald that glistens in the heart of the city (see page 12). Take a walk in the park, join the march of strollers under a green canopy of trees and hobnob with the rich and famous, or at least their au pairs. Stop to people-watch at Bethesda Terrace or watch model boats cruise the pond close to East 72nd Street. Further down is the old-fashioned Carousel. Stop at the **Dairy** (❶ (212) 794 6564) for park information or to buy a poster. ❶ (212) 360 3444 Ⓦ www.centralparknyc.org Ⓝ Bus: 1, 2, 3, 4 to 64th St; Subway: N, R to Fifth Ave–59th St; 4, 5, 6 to 86th St ❶ There are multiple entrances to the park. These are east side public transport options

Wildlife Conservation Society's Central Park Zoo

Nobody's on a diet over at the Polar Zone, where Gus and Ida prowl their rocky habitat for peanut-butter balls. These polar bears are

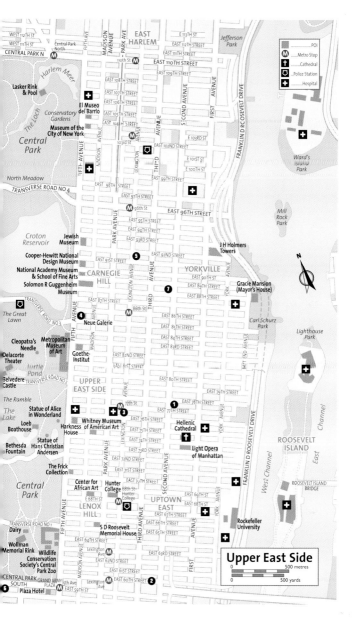

HIGH-RISE HAWK

It may be tough getting into one of the privileged and very pricey mansions on Fifth Avenue, but no one – that means no one – gets evicted. So it came as a big surprise to Pale Male, a red-tailed hawk, when he and partner, Lola, were ousted from their precarious coop on the 12th-storey ledge of 927 Fifth in December 2004. Pale Male had been mating on his perch for a decade under the careful watch of binocular-bearing bird lovers. He even gained celebrity status as the star of a film, *Pale Male*, made possible by Frederic Lilien, who kept a six-year vigil on the hawk. Protesters against the hawks' eviction, including Mary Tyler Moore, dressed up as birds and waved placards reading 'Honk for Hawks', and passing cabbies and bus drivers often complied. It all came to a peaceful resolution when building owners bowed to environmentalists and constructed a nesting platform. Pale Male returned to his perch, and he and Lola can sometimes be seen nearby, frolicking on Woody Allen's balcony. Ⓦ www.palemale.com

experienced divers, too. You can also visit the Tropic Zone, which houses a fantastic collection of tropical birds, and the Temperate Territory, which includes the California sea lion tank. The sea lion quartet feeding (at 11.30, 14.00 and 16.00) is popular. ❷ 64th St & Fifth Ave ❶ (212) 439 6500 Ⓦ www.centralparkzoo.com ◐ 10.00–17.00 Mon–Fri, 10.00–17.30 Sat & Sun (22 Mar–2 Nov); 10.00–16.30 (3 Nov–21 Mar) Ⓝ Bus: 1, 2, 3, 4 to 64th St; Subway: N, R to Fifth Ave; 6 to 68th St–Hunter College ❶ Admission charge

CULTURE

Philanthropic New Yorkers bequeathed their mansions and art collections to New York by establishing some of the world's most wonderful museums on Museum Mile (see page 18). Several other not to be missed museums are also located in this area.

Cooper-Hewitt National Design Museum

Housed in Andrew Carnegie's 'modest' mansion, Cooper-Hewitt is an extension of the Smithsonian Institution. Its permanent collections explore both contemporary and historical design, from graphics to decorative arts, with large exhibits of textiles and even wallpaper. Some changing exhibits are sharp and cutting-edge; others are presented with a sense of humour. ❷ 2 E 91st St ❶ (212) 849 8400 ❾ www.cooperhewitt.org ❹ 10.00–17.00 Mon–Fri, 10.00–18.00 Sat, 11.00–18.00 Sun ❾ Subway: 4, 5, 6 to 86th St ❶ Admission charge

The Frick Collection

If you visit the Frick, as aficionados fondly call it, you'll immediately add it to your shortlist of favourite museums, mainly because it's small enough to see in a day, and the collection is the ultimate in high quality. Stroll through the elegant beaux arts home, relishing exquisite 18th-century French furniture, oriental rugs, porcelains and enamels. You'll get a sense of what it was like when Henry Clay Frick actually lived in this mansion. Relax for a moment at the courtyard atrium, then continue your journey through the 18 galleries gazing at some of the world's most famous paintings: Renoir's *Mother and Children*, Romney's *Lady Hamilton as 'Nature'*, or El Greco's magnificent, red-robed *St Jerome*. Don't miss the old master European painters,

including Rembrandt, Titian, Gainsborough and Vermeer. ⓐ 1 E 70th St
ⓣ (212) 288 0700 ⓦ www.frick.org ⓛ 10.00–18.00 Tues–Sat, 11.00–17.00
Sun, closed Mon ⓝ Subway: 6 to 68th St–Hunter College
ⓘ Admission charge

Metropolitan Museum of Art

The magnificent Met, as it is known to New Yorkers, has permanent
collections representing every corner of the earth and every era. The
museum is so vast that you could explore the art here for several
months (or years). Start at the reflecting pool in front of the Egyptian
Nubian Temple of Dendur (circa 15 BC), decorated with elegant sandstone
reliefs (and some 19th-century graffiti!). The Met is organised in sections,
easily reached from its neoclassical Great Hall. European masters
are represented by El Greco's *View of Toledo*, or Titian's *Venus and the
Lute Player*. The American collection is large and varied. The Met was
a latecomer to modern art, but there is a healthy collection of works
from Pablo Picasso to Jackson Pollock (see the Whitney and MoMA,
pages 90 and 66, for larger modern collections). To satisfy hunger
pangs, there are several cafés; be sure to view the skyline from the
Roof Garden (ⓛ May–late autumn), or have cocktails and appetisers
at the **Balcony Bar** while enjoying live chamber music (ⓛ 16.00–20.30
Fri & Sat). ⓐ 1000 Fifth Ave ⓣ (212) 535 7710 ⓦ www.metmuseum.org
ⓛ 09.30–17.30 Tues–Thur & Sun, 09.30–21.00 Fri & Sat, closed Mon
ⓝ Subway: 4, 5, 6 to 86th St ⓘ Admission charge

Solomon R Guggenheim Museum

Frank Lloyd Wright is the first artist you meet as you gaze upon
his curvaceous building that sits on Fifth Avenue at 89th Street.
Wright felt that New York was 'overbuilt, overpopulated, and lacked
architectural merit'. Despite his disenchantment, and even his death

before its completion, the controversial structure is a monument to Wright's boundless talent, and an icon of 20th-century modernist architecture. Under a soaring glass dome, a continuous ramp slopes gently downwards passing the various collections of Solomon R Guggenheim. Ongoing exhibits include works of prominent artists, including Klee, Picasso, Chagall and Kandinsky. Photography is seen through the eyes of Robert Mapplethorpe. The collection includes art styles from Pollock's abstracts to Post-Impressionist Van Gogh.

🅰 1071 Fifth Ave 🆃 (212) 423 3500 🆆 www.guggenheim.org

🕒 10.00–17.45 Sun–Wed & Fri, 10.00–19.45 Sat, closed Thur

Ⓝ Subway: 4, 5, 6 to 86th St ⓘ Admission charge

🔺 *The bustling Metropolitan Museum of Art*

Whitney Museum of American Art

Established in 1931 by Gertrude Vanderbilt Whitney, who worked as a sculptor and amassed artworks of friends, the museum's collection of 20th-century American art is considered one of the best. Housed in an appropriately modern building, the Whitney exhibits art from 1900 to the present. ⓐ 945 Madison Ave ① (212) 570 3600 ⓦ www.whitney.org ⓛ 11.00–18.00 Wed & Thur, Sat & Sun, 13.00–21.00 Fri, closed Mon & Tues ⓝ Bus: M1, M2, M3, M4 to 74th St; Subway: 6 to 77th St ① Admission charge

RETAIL THERAPY

Madison Avenue shopping means high prices for high cheekbones. Start at **Barney's** (ⓐ 660 Madison Ave ① (212) 826 8900 ⓦ www.barneys.com ⓛ 10.00–20.00 Mon–Fri, 10.00–19.00 Sat, 11.00–18.00 Sun), then cruise by **Valentino** (ⓐ 747 Madison Ave

⬥ No escape from the steel architectural add-ons

🛈 (212) 772 6969 🕘 10.00–18.00 Mon–Sat, closed Sun), **Dolce & Gabbana** (🄰 825 Madison Ave 🛈 (212) 249 4100 🕘 10.00–18.00 Mon–Wed, Fri & Sat, 10.00–19.00 Thur, 12.00–17.00 Sun) and **Carolina Herrera** (🄰 954 Madison Ave 🛈 (212) 249 6552 🕘 10.00–18.00 Mon–Sat, closed Sun). Head further east for less pricey places, such as **Cantaloup** (🄰 1036 Lexington Ave 🛈 (212) 249 3566 🕘 10.00–19.00 Mon–Sat, 11.00–18.00 Sun) and **Pookie & Sebastian** (🄰 1448 Second Ave 🛈 (212) 861 0550 🕘 11.00–21.00 Mon–Sat, 11.00–19.00 Sun). Also look for discount designer duds at thrift stores around Third Avenue.

Bloomingdales Bloomie's is the adored Art Deco department store of the east side, and it has never lost its panache. It's well worth browsing. You'll find designer as well as mid-priced items, and a broad selection of menswear. 🄰 1000 Third Ave 🛈 (212) 705 2000 🌐 www.bloomingdales.com 🕘 10.00–20.30 Mon–Fri, 10.00–19.00 Sat, 11.00–19.00 Sun 🚇 Subway: 4, 5, 6 to 59th St; N, R to Lexington Ave–59th St

The Corner Bookstore A place for bookworms, this tiny shop's staff are known for their friendliness. Alongside its travel, classics and children's books is a neighbourly bulletin board advising where to find dog-walkers or learn a foreign language. 🄰 1313 Madison Ave 🛈 (212) 831 3554 🕘 10.00–20.00 Mon–Thur, 10.00–19.00 Fri, 11.00–18.00 Sat & Sun 🚇 Subway: 6 to 96th St

TAKING A BREAK

Orwasher's Bakery £ ❶ Third-generation bakers make rye and pumpernickel bread the old-fashioned way – by hand, then baked in a brick-hearth oven. Pick up a loaf and picnic alongside the

East River at Carl Schurz Park. ⓐ 308 E 78th St ⓣ (212) 288 6569
ⓦ www.orwasherbakery.com ⓛ 07.00–19.00 Mon–Sat, 09.00–16.00
Sun ⓝ Subway: 4, 5, 6 to 77th St

Serendipity 3 £ ❷ Re-energise yourself with a Frrrozen Hot Chocolate
at this whimsical ice-cream parlour that also serves a full lunch and
dinner menu of sandwiches, casseroles, omelettes, pastas and seafood.
ⓐ 225 E 60th St ⓣ (212) 838 3531 ⓛ 11.30–24.00 Sun–Thur, 11.30–01.00
Fri, 11.30–02.00 Sat ⓝ Subway: N, R to Lexington Ave–59th St

Soup Burg £ ❸ This coffee shop and burger boutique is low on décor but
comes highly recommended by neighbourhood locals. ⓐ 1055 Lexington
Ave ⓣ (212) 734 6964 ⓛ 05.00–23.00 ⓝ Subway: 4, 5, 6 to 77th St

Café Sabarsky ££ ❹ Housed in an elegant town house once occupied
by Grace Vanderbilt and on the lower floor of the jewel-box Neue
Galerie (see page 20), this authentic café serves imported Viennese
coffee piled high with *schlag* (whipped cream), accompanied by
pastries to rival any served in Vienna. Try the apple strudel or the
Klimt torte, a hazelnut cake layered with bittersweet chocolate. A full
lunch menu is also available. It's pricey here, but cheaper than a ticket
to Austria ⓐ 1048 Fifth Ave ⓣ (212) 288 0665
ⓦ www.cafesabarsky.com ⓛ 09.00–18.00 Mon & Wed, 09.00–21.00
Thur–Sun, closed Tues ⓝ Subway: 4, 5, 6 to 86th St

AFTER DARK

RESTAURANTS

Sfoglia ££ ❺ People book reservations six weeks in advance to
dine at this chic Italian eatery. The menu, influenced by Renaissance

recipes with an emphasis on local ingredients, changes twice a month. If the dinner wait is too long, try lunch. ⓐ 1402 Lexington Ave ⓘ (212) 831 1402 ⓦ www.sfogliarestaurant.com ⓛ 12.00–14.30 Tues–Sat, 17.30–23.00 Mon–Sat, closed Sun ⓝ Subway: 6 to 96th St

Aureole £££ ⓰ Situated in a brownstone building, with rooms full of fresh flowers, you can experience Charlie Palmer's progressive American cuisine. On a budget? Try the *prix fixe* menu. ⓐ 135 W 42nd St ⓘ (212) 319 1660 ⓦ www.charliepalmer.com ⓛ 12.00–14.30 Mon–Sat, 17.00–22.30 Sun–Thur, 17.00–23.00 Fri & Sat ⓝ Subway: N, R to 59th St–Lexington Ave

Elaine's £££ ⓻ The restaurant of New York's favourite hostess has become an institution. It started with her literary friends and soon the world's celebs were hanging out in this unassuming place. The food's great, too. ⓐ 1703 Second Ave ⓘ (212) 534 8103 ⓛ 18.00–02.00 Mon–Sat, 17.00–01.00 Sun ⓝ Subway: 4, 5, 6 to 86th St

BARS & CLUBS

The Carlyle This joint is alive with music. Stop by Bemelmans Bar for its relaxed atmosphere and drinks, and enjoy whimsical murals by satirist Ludwig Bemelman, creator of the *Madeleine* book series. If you're in for an evening of intimate cabaret, the Café Carlyle hosts a variety of entertainers, including Woody Allen with his New Orleans jazz band. Entertainment programmes vary in both the bar and café. ⓐ 35 E 76th St ⓘ (212) 744 1600 ⓦ www.thecarlyle.com ⓛ Bemelmans: 12.00–23.30 Mon–Fri, 12.00–00.30 Sat & Sun; Café Carlyle: 18.00–23.00 Mon–Sat, closed Sun ⓝ Subway: 6 to 77th St

Upper West Side & Harlem

The Upper West Side starts at Columbus Circle and 59th Street. It runs all along Central Park to 110th Street, just below Columbia University, and crosses to West End Avenue and Riverside Drive, overlooking the Hudson River.

Shaped like a pointing finger, at its long northern tip Manhattan narrows dramatically and is filled with greenscapes and stunning views. From here, the **George Washington Bridge** spans the Hudson and sparkles elegantly at dusk like a diamond necklace. The Upper West Side is filled with churches and important museums; trendy spots are popping up everywhere. There's a burgeoning interest in the more northerly neighbourhoods such as Harlem and Washington Heights.

SIGHTS & ATTRACTIONS

Elegant Art Deco and beaux arts buildings line Central Park West. The **Dakota** (❷ Central Park West & W 72nd St), noteworthy as the first large apartment house there, and for its famous couple, Yoko Ono and John Lennon, was built by Henry J Hardenbergh, who also built The Plaza Hotel (see page 44). Known as an intellectual and artistic neighbourhood, with tree-lined streets and classic brownstones, the Upper West Side is home to several museums and the phenomenal Lincoln Center complex (see page 100).

It is down the beautiful Central Park West that the world-famous giant balloons float some four storeys tall on their way to Macy's department store (see page 22) each Thanksgiving Day. If you go, arrive early and dress warmly.

Cathedral of St John the Divine

Still the world's largest Gothic cathedral, this is a religious and cultural centre with a modern attitude. Stained-glass windows depict sports, American history, medicine and religious subjects. Carved statues of saints adorn the High Altar, but there are also likenesses of Christopher Columbus and Abraham Lincoln. Then there's the live elephant in the processional on St Francis Day. ⓐ 1047 Amsterdam Ave ⓣ (212) 316 7490 ⓦ www.stjohndivine.org ⓛ 07.00–18.00 Mon–Sat, 07.00–19.00 Sun ⓢ Subway: 1 to 110th St–Cathedral Parkway

Columbus Circle

New York's only roundabout, a kind of revolving door between midtown and New York's cultural epicentre, is a tangle of traffic surrounded by skyscrapers. The Donald's (Trump, of course) Hotel towers over the circle, but it's the all-glass, glitzy, Time-Warner Center that draws crowds. Its mall, more prosaically known as **The Shops** (ⓦ www.shopsatcolumbuscircle.com), brings 40 brand-name stores and top designers to the neighbourhood, including Cartier, Williams-Sonoma and Thomas Pink. Trendy but pricey restaurants top the list of numerous eateries. Come here mid-morning on Sunday, when traffic is non-existent, and enjoy the beauty of the circle and its statue of Columbus. ⓐ Crossroads of Broadway, Central Park West & Central Park South (59th St)

Hip hop tours

See where it all began. Old-school emcee legends lead a variety of bus and walking tours through Harlem and other influential neighbourhoods, showcasing the cultural phenomenon that is hip hop. ⓣ (212) 714 3527 ⓦ www.hushtours.com

◯ The Robert F Kennedy Bridge, seen below the Hell Gate Bridge

CULTURE

American Museum of Natural History

Every true New Yorker has spent time on the learning curve in this sprawling museum that ambitiously sets out to cover everything in creation. Dinosaur delirium is alive and well in the vaulted rotunda, where a barosaurus skeleton stands 152 m (500 ft) high on its hind legs. More dinosaurs and pterodactyls with scientific names too long to remember occupy three large halls in the museum.

Highlights include dioramas that trace Asian, African and South American peoples alongside others depicting frozen-in-time animal life. The Hall of Ocean Life exhibits a 28.5-m (94-ft) blue whale. There's a massive meteorite and Santiago Calatrava's stainless-steel Time Capsule. In the ultra-modern Rose Center for Earth and Space you can see the Planetarium sphere and the *Cosmic Collisions* space show. Here, too, is an IMAX theatre. ⓐ 79th St at Central Park West ⓣ (212) 769 5100 ⓦ www.amnh.org ⓛ 10.00–17.45 ⓝ Subway: B, C to 81st St

Apollo Theater

'Where Stars are Born and Legends are Made'™, the legendary Apollo Theater helped to put black music into America's mainstream. Among those discovered at the Apollo were musical greats such as Ella Fitzgerald, Aretha Franklin and Count Basie. Wednesday's Amateur Night, which showcases young talent in competition, is a hoot. ⓐ 253 W 125th St ⓣ (212) 531 5300 ⓦ www.apollotheater.org ⓛ Box office & gift shop: 10.00–18.00 Mon–Sat, closed Sun ⓝ Subway: 1 to 125th St

The Cloisters

Step back into medieval times with a visit to The Cloisters, high on a hill over the Hudson River. The collection, which is part of the

HARLEM

When southern black people migrated north, Harlem was their destination. They brought vitality to the area, especially during the Harlem Renaissance, a golden era of literature and the arts (1919–29). It was a time when the city became known as 'The Big Apple'; the place was rocking and the sound of jazz flowed through the air. Black Americans brought their religion and built many churches, and they also brought their soul food and established a bustling society.

Stroll through the area and wonder at the mix of grandiose brownstones and dingy tenements. Places to see include lovely row houses in Hamilton Heights (also known as Sugar Hill), once home to Sugar Ray Robinson. Striver's Row has elegant Sanford White-designed town homes – the word on the street is 'Move over, SoHo: here comes Harlem'.

Hunt for bargains at the Malcolm Shabazz market (see page 23), stop on 125th Street at Malcolm X Corner, and don't miss the **Studio Museum** (⑧ 144 W 125th St ① (212) 864 4500 ⑩ www.studiomuseum.org ① 12.00–18.00 Wed–Fri & Sun, 10.00–20.00 Sat, closed Mon & Tues), showcasing art by African Americans and artists of African descent. More music and entertainment? You can't go wrong with the Apollo Theater (see opposite) or a gospel service at the **Abyssinian Baptist Church** (⑨ W 138th St).

Metropolitan Museum of Art, features art and architecture from the Middle Ages. Stained glass, enamels, icons and the famous Belgian Unicorn tapestries are on exhibition. The exquisite

12th-century Cuxa Cloister, with its pink marble columns from a French abbey, surrounds a square flower garden. ➋ Fort Tryon Park ➊ (212) 923 3700 Ⓦ www.metmuseum.org Ⓛ 09.30–16.45 Tues–Sun, closed Mon (Nov–end Feb); 09.30–17.15 Tues–Sun, closed Mon (Mar–end Oct) Ⓝ Bus: M4 to The Cloisters; Subway: A to 190th St

Lincoln Center for the Performing Arts

In its relatively short life, Lincoln Center has grown to include everything from the 'a' in aria to the 'z' in jazz. In one central place, it includes the acoustically unsurpassed Alice Tully Hall (chamber music), the Avery Fisher Hall, the Metropolitan Opera House, the New York City Ballet, the New York City Opera, the New York Philharmonic Orchestra, the New York State Theater, the Vivian Beaumont Theater, the Walter Reade Theater for the centre's film society, the Juilliard School of Music, a library and a museum. In winter, the Big Apple Circus pitches its tents on the centre's huge plaza. Best of all, when summer comes, the plaza is transformed into a swinging spot full of music, where New Yorkers and visitors come to dance the night away. ➋ 70 Lincoln Center Plaza (Broadway at W 64th St) ➊ (212) 875 5456 Ⓦ www.lincolncenter.org Ⓝ Subway: 1 to 66th St

Museum of Arts & Design

You'll find objects made of clay, fibre, glass, metal and wood – celebrated as much for their function as for their artistic concept and design. Exhibits also expand into architecture, fashion, interior design, performing arts and technology. ➋ 2 Columbus Circle ➊ (212) 299 7777 Ⓦ www.madmuseum.org Ⓛ 11.00–18.00 Tues, Wed & Fri–Sun, 11.00–21.00 Thur, closed Mon Ⓝ Subway: 1, 9 to 66th St ➊ Admission charge

Strawberry Fields, Central Park

The Beatles' song *Strawberry Fields Forever* inspired this garden of peace to honour John Lennon, who died a tragic death at the hands of a fanatic fan. The tear-shaped park, chosen by John's wife, Yoko Ono, was one of Lennon's favourite spots. A simple mosaic, based on one

⬤ *Imagine: the talent the world can't forget*

from Pompeii, bears the single word *IMAGINE*, the title of another Lennon song. Visitors walk under shady trees along curving paths, and pay their respects. ⓐ Central Park – W 71st to 74th Sts Ⓦ www.centralparknyc.org

TAKING A BREAK

You can get some fresh air over near the Hudson River at the 79th Street Boat Basin. Or stop at one of the area's famous delis – Zabars, for example, at 80th Street and Broadway (see page 26).

Good Enough to Eat £ ❶ This all-American comfort-food eatery offers a feast on a healthy platter of pancakes, bacon and eggs, or try the speciality pumpkin-bread toast. ⓐ 483 Amsterdam Ave ⓣ (212) 496 0163 Ⓦ www.goodenoughtoeat.com Ⓛ 08.00–22.30 Mon–Thur, 08.00–23.00 Fri, 09.00–23.00 Sat, 09.00–22.00 Sun Ⓝ Subway: 1 to 79th St; B, C to 81st St

Gray's Papaya £ ❷ The greatest $1.25 hot dog in town – wash it down with papaya juice. ⓐ 2090 Broadway ⓣ (212) 799 0243 Ⓛ 24 hours Ⓝ Subway: B, C, 1 to 72nd St

Magnolia Bakery £ ❸ The headquarters of cupcakes. ⓐ 200 Columbus Ave ⓣ (212) 724 8101 Ⓦ www.magnoliabakery.com Ⓛ 08.00–22.00 Sun–Thur, 08.00–24.00 Fri & Sat Ⓝ Subway: B, C, 1, 2, 3 to 72nd St

Sylvia's £ ❹ Finger-lickin' soul food at its best. Be sure to try the Queen's collard greens, tender ribs and candied yams. ⓐ 328 Lenox Ave ⓣ (212) 996 0660 Ⓦ www.sylviassoulfood.com Ⓛ 08.00–22.30 Mon–Sat, 11.00–20.00 Sun Ⓝ Subway: 2, 3 to 125th St

AFTER DARK

Most restaurants around Lincoln Center offer an early start for dinner, giving customers plenty of time to eat and make it to the theatre in time for the performance. There are restaurants offering food from a huge variety of international cuisines, as well as soul food in Harlem.

RESTAURANTS

Awash £ ❺ Casual Ethiopian fare such as tasty *gomen besiga*: sautéed beef, collard greens, onions and just a bit of cardamom. ⓐ 947 Amsterdam Ave ⓣ (212) 961 1416 ⓦ www.awashnyc.com ⓛ 13.00–24.00 Mon–Fri, 12.00–24.00 Sat & Sun Ⓝ Subway: 1 to 103rd St

Kefi £ ❻ A real favourite, Kefi serves casual yet delicious Greek food at reasonable prices. ⓐ 505 Columbus Ave ⓣ (212) 873 0200 ⓦ www.kefirestaurant.com ⓛ 17.00–22.00 Sun–Thur, 17.00–23.00 Fri & Sat Ⓝ Subway: 1 to 86th St

Petrossian £££ ❼ This ornate restaurant entices gourmets with beluga, ostera and sevruga caviar. ⓐ 182 W 58th St & 7th Ave ⓣ (212) 245 2214 ⓦ www.petrossian.com ⓛ 11.30–15.00 daily, 17.30–23.00 Mon–Sat, 17.30–22.30 Sun Ⓝ Subway: N, R to 57th St

BARS & CLUBS

Lenox Lounge Billie Holiday, Miles Davis and John Coltrane all played at this historic Art Deco club – a fixture since 1939. Jazz and dinner nightly. ⓐ 288 Lenox Ave (Malcom X Boulevard) ⓣ (212) 427 0253 ⓦ www.lenoxlounge.com ⓛ 12.00–04.00 Ⓝ Subway: 2, 3 to 125th St

Greenwich Village

In the 1820s, wealthy downtowners fled to the Village, escaping a bustling, bawdy metropolis. When the Village grew, they fled further uptown. A century or so later, counter-culture uptowners reversed gears. Bohemians, free-thinkers, artists and poets came downtown to the quiet charm of this now historical area.

For many years, Greenwich Village differentiated between the East Village and the West Village. Nowadays that division is fuzzy, but one thing's for sure: Greenwich Village starts at Washington Square Arch and around sprawling New York University. Fortunately, as a historical landmark district, the Village is protected. People come to wander – slipping into cosy restaurants and hunting for little treasures. As dusk settles in, they look for good theatre and the thrill of thrashing around to techno music until dawn.

SIGHTS & ATTRACTIONS

It's both easy and delightful to get lost along the lovely, tree-lined streets that wind, without rhyme or reason, through the fabric of the Village. It's a place that twists and turns – where West 10th crosses West 4th, and Waverly crosses Waverly (yes, it's a fact!).

CULTURE

In contrast to the city's huge, uptown museums, the Village is full of art galleries and small collections. But don't be fooled; the quality here is unrivalled.

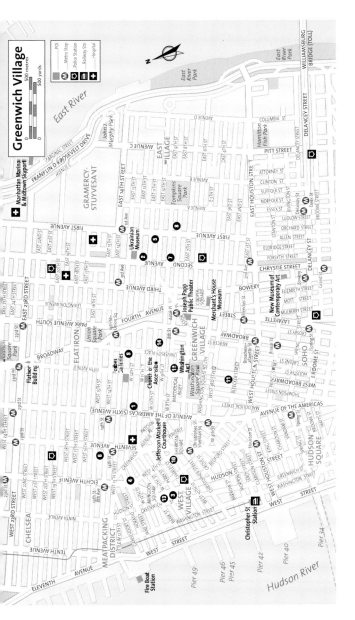

ARCHITECTURE, ARTISTS & AUTHORS

In a swampy wasteland far north of Wall Street there was a gallows at the Hanging Elm in the 1800s. The spot had been a paupers' burial ground, as well as a duelling ground. It was incomprehensible at the time that this square would eventually be surrounded by elegant 19th-century town houses. The Washington Square Arch designed by Stanford White (modelled after Paris's Arc de Triomphe) was erected there to mark the centenary of George Washington's inauguration. It is the unofficial symbol of New York University, which surrounds the area, and marks the downtown end of Fifth Avenue, and the beginning of street confusion. One snowy eve in 1917, the arch was the scene of a raucous party when six revellers climbed to the top to declare Greenwich Village 'a free and independent republic'.

Washington Square Park has its share of literary and artistic history. Edward Hopper lived at No 3, one of the remaining Greek Revival row houses. Henry James visited his grandmother there, subsequently naming a novel *Washington Square*. The park has jettisoned its drug dealers in favour of impromptu musicians, a few chess hustlers and skateboarders. An art show takes place here in spring and autumn, under the watchful eye of the ageing Hanging Elm.

A turreted, 1876 Victorian-Gothic structure, **Jefferson Market Courthouse** (📍 425 Sixth Ave ☎ (212) 243 4334 🕐 09.00–20.00 Mon & Wed, 10.00–18.00 Tues & Thur, 10.00–17.00 Fri & Sat, closed Sun) is now a public library.

⬥ *Washington Square and Arch in Manhattan*

Surrounding one-time bordellos are now gift shops, cafés and a hairdresser. An elevated train ran along the avenue, then known as Lady's Mile. Patchin Place is easy to miss; the small cul-de-sac with ten Federal town houses was home to Theodore Dreiser, author of *An American Tragedy*, e e cummings and O Henry. Around the corner, on West 11th Street, is the triangular cemetery of the Spanish and Portuguese Synagogue; only a few headstones remain. Further along, a Greek Revival house was destroyed when a bomb made by the radical student group the Weathermen accidentally exploded; neighbour Dustin Hoffman escaped unharmed.

At the corner of West 10th Street on Fifth Avenue is the Richard Upjohn-designed **Church of the Ascension** (☎ (212) 254 8620 ⓦ www.ascensionnyc.org). Stanford White commissioned Louis Comfort Tiffany and John LaFarge stained-glass windows for the church. Federal-style 77 Bedford Street is the oldest house in the Village. Next door is New York's narrowest house, which measures less than 3 m (10 ft) in width. Louisa May Alcott wrote *Little Women* while living at Nos 130–132 MacDougal, and the Provincetown Playhouse premiered many of Eugene O'Neill's plays.

The east side of the Village also has architectural treasures, many associated with the John Jacob Astor Family. On Lafayette Street is Colonnade Row (No 428), once occupied by Astors and Vanderbilts, and the Puck Building (No 295), which housed the German-language magazine *Puck*. The Public Theater was originally the Astor Library (No 425, see page 116).

Forbes Magazine Galleries

The passion of magazine magnate Malcolm Forbes is the basis for the idiosyncratic collection in this petite museum. Among the exhibits are 10,000 marching toy soldiers in battle, presidential papers, Abraham Lincoln's stovepipe hat, and early versions of the Monopoly game. An exhibition of jewellery collections of famous people includes the Scorpio Pendant that belonged to Princess Grace. ⓐ 62 Fifth Ave ⓣ (212) 206 5548 ⓦ www.forbesgalleries.com ⓛ 10.00–16.00 Tues, Wed, Fri & Sat, Thur for group tours only, closed Sun & Mon ⓢ Subway: R to 8th St; F, M to 14th St

Merchant's House Museum

By virtue of remaining in one family, the house built for Seabury Tredwell in 1832 is New York's only fully intact Federalist home – inside and out. Left to the city by the wealthy merchant's eighth child, it contains many of the family's original furniture, memorabilia, their period clothing, and even needlework and family photographs. ⓐ 29 E 4th St ⓣ (212) 777 1089 ⓦ www.merchantshouse.com ⓛ 12.00–17.00 Thur–Mon, closed Tues & Wed ⓢ Subway: N, R to 8th St; 6 to Astor Pl; B, F to Broadway–Lafayette St

RETAIL THERAPY

Thanks to low-rise architecture, the Village is filled with small stores, often with unique and one-of-a-kind items. The further east the shop, the funkier things get. There are plenty of places for body piercing or tattoos, if that's your pleasure. A permanent street market has taken over 8th Street at Third Avenue. There's no real menu of products, but expect good finds in used vinyl. Some designer stores have moved in, especially on the northwestern end of Bleecker Street where the likes of Ralph Lauren and Marc Jacobs have set up shop.

C O Bigelow The customer comes first at this 170-year-old store, where hand-milled soaps, old-fashioned toothpaste and ancient (but currently trendy) homeopathic remedies are sold.
🅰 414 Sixth Ave 🕐 (212) 533 2700 🔵 www.bigelowchemists.com
🕐 07.30–21.00 Mon–Fri, 08.30–19.00 Sat, 08.30–17.30 Sun
🅝 Subway: R to 8th St; F to 14th St

Marc Jacobs The designer's edgy style in his more affordable line, Marc by Marc, includes collections for both genders. Three stores – men's, women's and accessories – are clustered on Bleecker Street.
🅰 403 Bleecker St 🕐 (212) 924 0026 🔵 www.marcjacobs.com
🕐 12.00–20.00 Mon–Sat, 12.00–19.00 Sun 🅝 Subway: A, C, E to 14th St; L to Eighth Ave

Strand Book Store A treasure chest filled with miles of review and second-hand books, sold at super-bargain prices. Specialities include collectables, hard-to-find and rare books. 🅰 828 Broadway
🕐 (212) 473 1452 🔵 www.strandbooks.com 🕐 09.30–22.30 Mon–Sat, 11.00–22.30 Sun 🅝 Subway: L, N, Q, R, 4, 5, 6 to 14th St–Union Sq

TAKING A BREAK

New Yorkers love to people-watch. With all the pavement cafés, squares and parks, Greenwich Village is the perfect place to sit back, don a pair of sunglasses, and watch the fashion show. If you're lucky, you might even spot one of the many celebrities who call the Village their home.

Joe Jr. £ ❶ Grab a quick bite in the quintessential family-owned diner, great for burgers and Greek specials. Lots of regulars and 'hey-I'm-normal' celebs. **ⓐ** 482 Sixth Ave **ⓣ** (212) 924 5220 **ⓛ** 06.00–01.00 **Ⓝ** Subway: F, L, M, 1, 2, 3 to 14th St

⬥ *The Strand Book Store is home to 29 km (18 miles) of books*

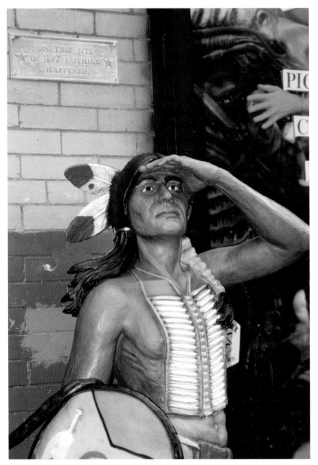

ON THIS SITE
IN 1897 NOTHING
HAPPENED

🔵 *Standing guard outside a place where 'nothing happened'*

Angelica Kitchen £–££ ❷ 'Strict veggies for vegans' has a huge following, lots of food and good value. Try the Dragon Bowl with rice, beans, tofu, steamed and sea veggies. ❸ 300 E 12th St
❶ (212) 228 2909 ⓦ www.angelicakitchen.com ⓛ 11.30–22.30
Ⓝ Subway: F to Second Ave

White Horse Tavern ££ ❸ Another literary relic is the 1880s pub frequented by Dylan Thomas, James Baldwin and Hunter S Thompson, among others. Refreshing pale ale is served in tall mugs. There is good bar food and outdoor seating. ❸ 567 Hudson St
❶ (212) 989 3956 ⓛ 11.00–02.00 Sun–Thur, 11.00–04.00 Fri & Sat
Ⓝ Subway: 1 to Christopher St–Sheridan Sq

AFTER DARK

In the West Village, jazz and Off-Broadway theatres share haunted streets, cafés and bars with ghosts of New York's literary and artistic past including greats from William Faulkner to Eugene O'Neill, Jimi Hendrix to Nina Simone. Over on the east side, curry and pierogi (boiled dumplings and sautéed onion with a filling) cohabit with vegetables and wraps. Among little enclaves of Ukrainian, Indian and Japanese eateries, stylish restaurants are moving in. Gentrification is a keyword in this area.

RESTAURANTS

Corner Bistro £ ❹ A holdout from the bohemian days of the West Village, the Corner Bistro is not to be missed. It serves arguably the best burger in New York City. ❸ 331 W 4th St
❶ (212) 242 9502 ⓛ 11.30–04.00 Mon–Sat, 12.00–04.00 Sun
Ⓝ Subway: A, C, E to Eighth Ave

Momofuku Noodle Bar £ ❺ Ramen, Korean buckwheat noodles and barbecue pork buns are served at a long wooden bar in the first of chef David Chang's East Village restaurants. Momofuku Ssäm Bar and Momofuku Ko are nearby. ⓐ 171 First Ave ❶ (212) 475 7899 🕐 12.00–23.00 Sun–Thur, 12.00–02.00 Fri & Sat ⓦ www.momofuku.com ⓝ Subway: F to Second Ave; L to First Ave; 6 to Astor Pl

La Nacional £ ❻ An unmarked door leads to unsurpassed paella in this very special Spanish spot. There are flamenco performances on Friday and Saturday and 'Tango Thursdays' (lessons between 19.00 and 21.30, dancing until 02.00). ⓐ 239 W 14th St ❶ (212) 243 9308 ⓦ www.tangolanacional.com 🕐 12.00–22.00 Sun–Wed, 12.00–23.00 Thur–Sat ⓝ Subway: A, C, E, F, L, M, 1, 2, 3 to 14th St

Veselka £ ❼ This Ukrainian diner is open around the clock. From breakfast to the après-club scene, expect queues out the door for its pierogi or kielbasa. Borscht or chilled soups follow the seasons. ⓐ 144 Second Ave ❶ (212) 228 9682 ⓦ www.veselka.com ⓝ Subway: 6 to Astor Pl

Yaffa Café £ ❽ The emphasis here is on healthy food and vegetarian dishes in a funky subterranean setting that's very much aimed at the after-hours crowd. It has an outdoor garden for summer dining. ⓐ 97 Saint Marks Pl ❶ (212) 674 9302 ⓦ www.yaffacafe.com 🕐 24 hours ⓝ Subway: L to First Ave; 6 to Astor Pl

Japonica ££ ❾ Fresh, high quality and large portions of sushi are the trademark of this restaurant that's popular with local regulars.

ⓐ 100 University Pl ⓣ (212) 243 7752 ⓦ www.japonicanyc.com
ⓛ 12.00–22.30 Mon–Thur, 12.00–23.00 Fri & Sat, 12.00–20.00 Sun
ⓝ Subway: L, N, R, 4, 5, 6 to 14th St–Union Sq

Mary's Fish Camp ££ ⓾ A tiny space serving titanic hunks of
succulence in super-fresh, lightly herbed lobster rolls. ⓐ 64 Charles St
ⓣ (646) 486 2185 ⓦ www.marysfishcamp.com ⓛ 12.00–15.00, 18.00–
23.00 Mon–Sat, closed Sun ⓝ Subway: 1, 9 to Christopher St–
Sheridan Sq

Massimo al Ponte Vecchio ££ ⓫ Chef Massimo Rellini brought his
Neapolitan accent and family cuisine from Italy. He cooks *zuppa di fagioli*
(cannellini bean soup with pasta) his mother's way. Tender venison loin
with balsamic vinegar sauce melts in the mouth. ⓐ 206 Thompson St
ⓣ (212) 228 7701 ⓦ www.massimonyc.com ⓛ 12.00–23.00 Sun–Thur,
12.00–23.30 Fri, 12.00–24.00 Sat ⓝ Subway: A, B, C, D, E, F, M to W 4th
St–Washington Sq

Otto Enoteca ££ ⓬ Tapas and new-wave pizza are griddle cooked in
an Italian train depot atmosphere. Choose between the marble-topped
standing tables or classic dining room. There's a younger crowd at
the weekend. ⓐ 1 Fifth Ave ⓣ (212) 995 9559 ⓦ www.ottopizzeria.com
ⓛ 11.30–24.00 ⓝ Subway: A, B, C, D, E, F, M to 4th St

Spotted Pig ££ ⓭ Trendy quasi-gastro pub has delicious
smoked trout and many Italian dishes. It became so crowded,
they opened a second floor. ⓐ 314 W 11th St ⓣ (212) 620 0393
ⓦ www.thespottedpig.com ⓛ 12.00–02.00 Mon–Fri, 11.00–02.00
Sat & Sun ⓝ L to Eighth Ave; A, C, M to 4th St; 1 to Christopher
St–Sheridan Sq

Il Cantinori £££ Northern Tuscan dishes are served in a romantic and relaxed atmosphere. The restaurant is decorated with stunning floral arrangements. It's a low-key favourite with locals and celebs. The magic is in the simplicity of such treats as *Petto D'Anatra con Lenticchie* (duck breast with lentils). ⓐ 32 E 10th St ⓣ (212) 673 6044 ⓦ www.ilcantinori.com ⓛ 12.00–14.30 Mon–Fri, 17.00–23.30 Mon–Thur & Sun, 17.00–24.00 Fri & Sat ⓢ Subway: L, N, R, 4, 5, 6 to 14th St–Union Sq

CINEMAS & THEATRES

IFCCenter This art-house theatre is the place for independent film fans. ⓐ 323 Sixth Ave ⓣ (212) 924 7771 ⓦ www.ifccenter.com ⓢ Subway: A, B, C, D, E, F, M to 4th St

Joseph Papp Public Theater Half a dozen theatres produce a wide variety of award-winning plays, musicals and Shakespeare at low ticket prices or free. The Public opened with *Hair*, brought plays like *A Chorus Line* to Broadway, and vows to continue innovative cultural projects. It also offers cutting-edge art cinema. ⓐ 425 Lafayette St ⓣ (212) 539 8500 ⓦ www.publictheater.org ⓢ Subway: N, R to 8th St; 6 to Astor Pl

BARS & CLUBS

Arthur's Tavern It's been around long enough for the paint to fade, but that's just part of the charm. Monday's Dixieland band is always on the programme. Jazz outfits play other nights from 19.00 to 21.00, and then the crowd mellows away the night with blues or R&B. ⓐ 57 Grove St ⓣ (212) 675 6879 ⓦ www.arthurstavernnyc.com ⓛ 20.00–04.00 Sun & Mon, 18.30–04.00 Tues–Sat ⓢ Subway: 1 to Christopher St–Sheridan Sq

Bowlmor Can a 42-lane cavernous bowling alley be cutting-edge? Most definitely yes – Monday Night Strike special has glow-in-the-dark bowling with a live DJ beat all night long for $20. It's said that the Rolling Stones and Cameron Diaz have bowled here. ⓐ 110 University Pl ⓣ (212) 255 8188 ⓦ www.bowlmor.com ⓛ 16.00–02.00 Mon & Thur, 16.00–01.00 Tues & Wed, 16.00–03.30 Fri & Sat, 16.00–24.00 Sun ⓝ Subway: L, N, Q, R, 4, 5, 6 to 14th St–Union Sq

Decibel Sample *sake* in a graffiti-cluttered basement, but don't fret if it's hard to choose from the 60 brands of rice wine. Shrimp and seaweed titbits at the bar. ⓐ 240 E 9th St ⓣ (212) 979 2733 ⓦ www.sakebardecibel.com ⓛ 18.00–02.50 Mon–Sat, 18.00–00.50 Sun ⓝ Subway: 6 to Astor Pl

Joe's Pub An intimate cabaret venue that has showcased live music and emerging artists, ranging from international rock bands through the underground pop scene to East Village entertainers, or legends like Eartha Kitt. Dinner also served. ⓐ 425 Lafayette St ⓣ (212) 539 8778 ⓦ www.joespub.com ⓛ Dinner: 18.00–22.30 ⓝ Subway: N, R to 8th St; 6 to Astor Pl

KGB A red-walled literary hangout with a varied history – it's a prohibition-era bar turned Ukrainian socialist social club. Nightly readings – and drinks, too. ⓐ 85 E 4th St ⓣ (212) 505 3360 ⓦ www.kgbbar.com ⓛ 19.00 04.00 ⓝ Subway: F to Second Ave

Eclectic neighbourhoods

The soul of New York lies in its neighbourhoods. Over hundreds of years, ethnic groups gave New York its special character, integrating their culture wherever they lived and worked. Over time, forgotten areas were gradually 'rediscovered' by artists and intellectuals, who added their own creativity and personality to the mix. The Lower East Side, Chelsea, Union Square, SoHo and Tribeca (Triangle Below Canal) have all been transformed in recent years and catapulted into the limelight. The latest neighbourhood to receive a facelift is the Meatpacking District. Who could imagine that a bunch of shack-like warehouses, designed for meat hooks, would appear consummately attractive to hot designers, celebs and trend-setting chefs?

SIGHTS & ATTRACTIONS

Flatiron Building

This unusual 22-storey triangular building, reputed to have been the city's first skyscraper, is New York's sweetheart landmark.
ⓐ 175 Fifth Ave at Broadway ⓝ Subway: B, D, R, 1, 6 to 23rd St

Little Italy

The aroma of bakeries and pasta fills the air on Mulberry Street, where the Feast of San Gennaro takes place in September.
ⓦ www.littleitalynyc.com ⓝ Subway: F, M to Broadway–Lafayette St; N, R to Prince St; 6 to Spring St

Lower East Side

Historically an immigrant, working-class neighbourhood, this was the gateway to America some 200 years ago. Newcomers squeezed

into dismal, teeming tenements in the bustling area around Orchard Street. It soon became a historical Jewish area, and then a Latino neighbourhood. Today the tenements are still there, but the old, abysmal apartments are now duplex haunts of hipsters, trendy restaurants and upmarket boutiques, and new construction is springing up everywhere. Many shops are closed Saturday and open Sunday and vestiges of its Jewish past can still be found.
Ⓝ Subway: J, M, Z to Essex St; F to Delancey St

Museum at Eldridge Street

One of the few survivors of nearly 500 Lower East Side synagogues is this famous one on Eldridge Street, recently restored. Its façade and interior combine Gothic stained-glass windows with Moorish arches. A beautiful walnut ark is intricately hand-carved, and *trompe l'œil* murals fill the walls under high vaulted ceilings. Among the people who worshipped here were Dr Jonas Salk, inventor of the polio vaccine, and actor Edward G Robinson. ❷ 12 Eldridge St Ⓦ www.eldridgestreet.org ❶ (212) 219 0302 ❶ Tours: Sun–Thur 10.00–17.00 on the half hour, last tour at 15.00; closed Fri & Sat, Jewish & national holidays Ⓝ Subway: F to E Broadway; B, D to Grand St; N, R, 6 to Canal St

SoHo cast-iron buildings

Named for its location south of Houston Street, SoHo is home to a historical district filled with late 1800s cast-iron buildings. The king of Greene Street (Nos 72–76) is considered the finest of 50 elaborately decorated buildings along five cobblestone blocks. Nearby is the Art Nouveau queen of Greene Street (Nos 28–30). Two more architecturally notable buildings are on Broadway. The Little Singer Building (named after the sewing machine), a beaux arts

Eclectic neighbourhoods (Map 1)

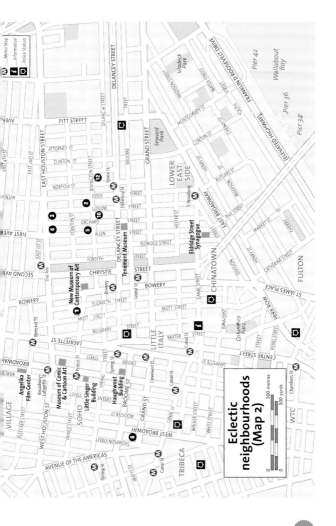

beauty at Nos 561–563, is an ornate terracotta structure adorned with wrought-iron balconies and dark green arches. The other is the Haughwout Building at Nos 488–491, with rows of arch-framed windows set on columns. These days the neighbourhood is filled with artists' lofts and art galleries. Subway: A, C, E, J, N, Q, R, 6 to Canal St

CULTURE

Downtown is immersed In art and culture. Slip into the landmark **Chelsea Hotel** (223 W 23 St (212) 243 3700 www.hotelchelsea.com Subway: C, E, 1 to 23rd St) to see its art-filled lobby. Emerging Tribeca artists hold a springtime event called **TOAST** (Tribeca Open Artist Studio Tour, www.toastartwalk.com), when locals open their basements, lofts and even rooftops to share their work with the public. SoHo is laughing with its **Museum of Comic and Cartoon Art** (594 Broadway, Suite 401 (212) 254 3511 www.moccany.org Subway: B, D, F, M to Broadway–Lafayette St; N, R to Prince St). Finally, do satisfy your curiosity with a look around the **Museum of Sex** (235 Fifth Ave (212) 689 6337 www.museumofsex.com 11.00–18.30 Sun–Fri, 11.00–20.00 Sat).

Galleries

While SoHo started the whole gallery thing, the scene has migrated to Chelsea, the Meatpacking District and the Lower East Side. The Meatpacking District has **Wooster Projects** (418 W 15th St (212) 871 6700 www.woosterprojects.com) with David Hockney and Andy Warhol pieces, and Chelsea has **Sonnabend** (536 W 22nd St (212) 627 1018 www.artnet.com/sonnabend.html), the **Paula Cooper Gallery** (534 W 21st St (212) 255 1105

◭ *Classic architecture of the Bowery Street area*

ⓦ www.paulacoopergallery.com) and **Gagosian** (ⓐ 555 W 24th St
ⓣ (212) 741 1111; ⓐ 522 W 21st St ⓣ (212) 741 1717
ⓦ www.gagosian.com).

New Museum of Contemporary Art

Towering over the Bowery like a wonky stack of cake boxes, the New
Museum's building is as much an attraction as the installations indoors.

🅐 235 Bowery 🕿 (212) 219 1222 🆆 www.newmuseum.org 🕐 12.00–18.00 Wed, Sat & Sun, 12.00–21.00 Thur & Fri, closed Mon & Tues Ⓝ Subway: 6 to Spring St; N, R to Prince St ❶ Admission charge

Rubin Museum of Art

Truly unique, this museum is dedicated to Himalayan art. 🅐 150 W 17th St 🕿 (212) 620 5000 🆆 www.rmanyc.org 🕐 11.00–17.00 Mon & Thur, 11.00–19.00 Wed, 11.00–22.00 Fri, 11.00–18.00 Sat & Sun, closed Tues Ⓝ Subway: 1 to 18th St; A, C, E to Eighth Ave; F to 14th St ❶ Admission charge

Tenement Museum

The experience of sweatshop garment workers and immigrants crammed into tiny quarters is relived in this preserved museum in an 1863 tenement house. The very popular interpretive tours visit different period apartments. 🅐 108 Orchard St 🕿 (212) 431 0233 🆆 www.tenement.org 🕐 10.00–18.00 Ⓝ Subway: F to Delancey St; B, D to Grand St; J, M, Z to Essex St ❶ Admission charge

RETAIL THERAPY

Shopping is an eclectic feast in these neighbourhoods, and the choices range from going mad with your credit card to happy haggling. In its mere 0.6 sq km (¼ sq mile), SoHo has its edgy haute couture and fun clothing, not to mention the famous art supply stores such as **Compleat Sculptor** (🅐 90 Vandam St 🕿 (212) 243 6074 🆆 www.sculpt.com) and **Pearl Paint** (🅐 308 Canal St 🕿 (212) 243 7932 🆆 www.pearlpaint.com). Further south in Tribeca and NoLita (north of Little Italy), gorgeous goodies include one-of-a-kind treasures found on Mulberry and Mott Streets. The Lower East Side has its share of boutiques, too, but you'll definitely want to seek out bargains in discount shops. Bargains can be had in Chelsea at **Loehmann's** (🄰 101 Seventh Ave 🄸 (212) 352 0856 🅦 www.loehmanns.com), but it's more of a chic boutique neighbourhood. Top designers are fast and furious in the Meatpacking District, but don't trip over a pavement vault-cover in your fancy new Jeffrey shoes.

17th Street Photo Hidden on the fourth floor, and tremendously flexible and customer-focused, this family-run business has all the latest camera and video goodies you could want. 🄰 33 W 17th St 🄸 (212) 366 9870 🅦 www.17photo.com 🄲 09.30–18.00 Mon–Fri, 10.00–16.00 Sun, closed Sat 🄼 Subway: F, L to 14th St; 1 to 18th St

ABC Carpet & Home An emporium of home furnishings from lighting to carpets and everything in between. 🄰 888 & 881 Broadway 🄸 (212) 473 3000 🅦 www.abchome.com 🄲 10.00–19.00 Mon–Wed &

⬯ *Funky paints adorn this doorway*

Sat, 10.00–20.00 Thur & Fri, 11.00–18.30 Sun Subway: N, R to 23rd St

Brooklyn Industries Fresh urban styles for men and women can be found at outlets of the local chain throughout Manhattan and Brooklyn. ⓐ 290 Lafayette St ⓣ (212) 219 0862 ⓦ www.brooklynindustries.com ⓛ 10.00–20.00 ⓝ Subway: B, D, F, M to Broadway–Lafayette St; N, R to Prince St

Diane von Furstenberg Her slinky, soft little wraps have been newsmakers for two decades. ⓐ 874 Washington St ⓣ (646) 486 4800 ⓦ www.dvf.com ⓛ 11.00–18.00 Mon & Fri, 11.00–19.00 Tues & Wed, 11.00–20.00 Thur, 11.00–17.00 Sat, 12.00–17.00 Sun ⓝ Subway: A, C, E to 14th St; L to Eighth Ave

Fishs Eddy Dishes, dishes and more dishes! Don't worry about lugging a suitcase full of saucers, cups and plates home – international shipping is available. ⓐ 889 Broadway ⓣ (212) 420 9020 ⓦ www.fishseddy.com ⓛ 10.00–22.00 Mon, 09.00–22.00 Tues–Sat, 10.00–21.00 Sun ⓝ Subway: N, R to 23rd St

Fragments An emporium showcasing 25 up-and-coming jewellery designers. ⓐ 116 Prince St ⓣ (212) 334 9588 ⓦ www.fragments.com ⓛ 10.00–17.00 Mon–Sat, 12.00–18.00 Sun ⓝ Subway: N, R to Prince St

Issey Miyake Sleek, shiny, silky, wearable art is worth a look in this high-tech Tribeca shop. ⓐ 119 Hudson St ⓣ (212) 226 0100 ⓦ www.isseymiyake.com ⓛ 11.00–19.00 Mon–Sat, 12.00–18.00 Sun ⓝ Subway: 1 to Franklin St

TAKING A BREAK

People-watch in Union Square, stop in for sourdough at City Bakery (🅐 3 W 18th St 🆆 www.thecitybakery.com), or grab a bite at a Lower East Side institution like **Yonah Schimmel Knishery**, where they've been baking savoury snacks since 1910 (🅐 137 E Houston St 🆃 (212) 477 2858 🆆 www.knishery.com 🕒 08.30–18.00 daily) or **Kossar's** (🅐 367 Grand St 🆃 (212) 253 2146 🆆 www.kossarsbialys.com 🕒 06.00–20.00 Mon–Thur & Sun, 06.00–14.00 Fri, closed Sat) for a bialy (cousin to a bagel).

Café Habana £ ❶ This eco-conscious, lively café serves up Latin fare. Try the Cuban sandwich and grilled Mexican corn. 🅐 17 Prince St 🆃 (212) 625 2001 🆆 www.ecoeatery.com 🕒 09.00–24.00 daily 🅝 Subway: N, R to Prince St

Economy Candy £ ❷ Sells a huge range of sweets. Look out for those molars! 🅐 108 Rivington St 🆃 (800) 352 4544 🆆 www.economycandy.com 🕒 09.00–18.00 Mon–Fri & Sun, 10.00–17.00 Sat 🅝 Subway: F to Delancey St; J, M, Z to Essex St

Katz's Delicatessen £ ❸ Katz's has been dishing out the best hand-cut pastrami and cured corned beef sandwiches since 1888. 🅐 205 E Houston St 🆃 (212) 254 2246 🆆 www.katzdeli.com 🕒 08.00–21.45 Mon & Tues, 08.00–22.45 Wed, Thur & Sun, 08.00–02.45 Fri & Sat 🅝 Subway: F to Second Ave

Russ & Daughters £ ❹ Specialising in caviar and smoked fish, the business is now in its fourth generation. 🅐 179 E Houston St 🆃 (212) 475 4880 🆆 www.russanddaughters.com 🕒 08.00–20.00 Mon–Fri, 09.00–17.00 Sat, 08.00–17.30 Sun 🅝 Subway: F to Second Ave

Teany Café £ ⑤ A teashop with a techno beat that has an all-day breakfast and vegetarian menu that includes vegan options. ⓐ 90 Rivington St ⓣ (212) 475 9190 ⓦ www.teany.com ⓛ 10.00–01.00 daily ⓝ Subway: F to Delancey St; J, M, Z to Essex St

Felix Bistro ££ ⑥ This bistro with a Brazilian flavour has outside seating and a welcoming atmosphere. ⓐ 340 W Broadway ⓣ (212) 431 0021 ⓦ www.felixnyc.com ⓛ 11.00–23.00 Sun & Mon, 11.00–24.00 Tues–Sat ⓝ Subway: A, C, E, J, N, R, Z, 1, 6, 9 to Canal St

AFTER DARK

These districts are for night owls. Trendy restaurants and bars pop up frequently (and disappear just as fast!). Besides the places listed here, see what's happening at **APT** (ⓐ 419 W 13th St ⓣ (212) 414 4245 ⓦ www.aptnyc.com), **Cielo** (ⓐ 18 Little W 12th St ⓣ (212) 645 5700), or **Hiro Ballroom** at the Maritime Hotel (ⓐ 88 Ninth Ave ⓣ (212) 625 8553 ⓦ www.hiroballroom.com). There are plenty of 24-hour restaurants around, just in case the urge for a nibble steals over you at some unexpected hour.

RESTAURANTS

Elephant and Castle £ ⑦ Reliable spot for comfort foods like burgers and omelettes. Long queues on weekends. ⓐ 68 Greenwich Ave, Seventh Ave & 11th St. ⓣ (212) 243 1400 ⓦ www.elephantandcastle.com ⓛ 08.30–24.00 Mon–Fri, 10.00–24.00 Sat & Sun ⓝ Subway: 1 to Rector St

Florent £ ⑧ Low-key French bistro food you can afford in this casual, fun place. ⓐ 69 Gansevoort St ⓣ (212) 989 5779

Ⓦ www.restaurantflorent.com Ⓛ 24 hours Ⓝ Subway: A, C, E to 14th St; L to Eighth Ave

Hill Country £ ❾ Sink your teeth into Texas-style barbecue in the middle of Manhattan. Ⓐ 30 W 26th St Ⓣ (212) 255 4544 Ⓦ www.hillcountryny.com Ⓛ 12.00–22.00 Sun–Wed, 12.00–23.00 Thur–Sat; bar is open until 02.00 nightly Ⓝ Subway: N, R to 28th St

Inoteca £ ❿ Italian tapas (oh, yes!), sandwiches and a hip wine bar. Ⓐ 98 Rivington St Ⓣ (212) 614 0473 Ⓦ www.inotecanyc.com Ⓛ 12.00–03.00 Mon–Fri, 10.00–03.00 Sat & Sun Ⓝ Subway: F to Delancey St; J, M, Z to Essex St

Republic £ ⓫ You'll find some of the best noodles outside of Chinatown right here. Ⓐ 37 Union Sq West Ⓣ (212) 627 7172 Ⓦ www.thinknoodles.com Ⓛ 11.30–22.30 Sun–Wed, 11.30–23.30 Thur–Sat Ⓝ Subway: L, N, Q, R, 4, 5, 6 to 14th St–Union Sq

Schiller's Liquor Bar £ ⓬ Come for a very late-night dinner in this French-bistro-esque space that's good for brunch as well. Ⓐ 131 Rivington St Ⓣ (212) 260 4555 Ⓦ www.schillersny.com Ⓛ 11.00–01.00 Mon–Wed, 11.00–02.00 Thur, 11.00–03.00 Fri, 10.00–03.00 Sat, 10.00–24.00 Sun Ⓝ Subway: F to Delancey St; J, M, Z to Essex St

Old Homestead ££ ⓭ This is the 'steak joint' to which New Yorkers from all quarters flock in order to feast on its delicious beef. Ⓐ 56 Ninth Ave Ⓣ (212) 242 9040 Ⓦ www.theoldhomesteadsteakhouse.com Ⓛ 12.00–22.45 Mon–Fri, 12.00–23.45 Sat, 01.00–21.45 Sun Ⓝ Subway: A, C, E to 14th St–Eighth Ave; L, 1, 2, 3 to 14th St

The Red Cat ££ Art adorns the barn-wood walls at this eclectic Chelsea joint, which has been frequented by locals for years. ⓐ 227 Tenth Ave ❶ (212) 242 1122 Ⓦ www.redcatrestaurants.com ❶ 17.00–23.00 Mon–Thur, 17.00–24.00 Fri & Sat, 17.00–22.00 Sun Ⓝ Subway: C, E to 23rd St

Union Square Café £££ Long popular with locals, who come for Michael Romano's dinner specials and the murals. ⓐ 21 E 16th St ❶ (212) 243 4020 Ⓦ www.unionsquarecafe.com ❶ 12.00–14.00 daily, 17.30–22.00 Sun Thur, 17.30–23.00 Fri & Sat Ⓝ Subway: L, N, Q, R, 6 to 14th St–Union Sq

CINEMAS & THEATRES
Angelika Film Center A place for artsy independent films. ⓐ 18 W Houston St ❶ (212) 995 2000 Ⓦ www.angelikafilmcenter.com ❶ Films start 10.45–24.00 Ⓝ Subway: B, D, F, Q to Broadway–Lafayette St; N, R to Prince St

BARS & CLUBS
Bowery Ballroom A rock-music venue in an old beaux arts building with state-of-the-art sound. ⓐ 6 Delancey St ❶ (212) 533 2111 Ⓦ www.boweryballroom.com ❶ 19.00–04.00 Ⓝ Subway: F to Second Ave; B, D to Grand St; J to Bowery; 6 to Spring St

Kenny's Castaways Bruce Springsteen played his first New York City show right here; live music most nights. ⓐ 157 Bleecker St ❶ (917) 475 1323 Ⓦ www.kennyscastaways.net ❶ Variable, according to show Ⓝ Subway: 6 to Bleecker St; C, E to W 4th St

❶ *The skyline of midtown Manhattan*

 OUT OF TOWN
trips

Brooklyn

Brooklyn Bridge was America's first steel suspension bridge, and thousands walk across its 1,834-m (6,016-ft) footbridge every day. The views across to Manhattan are nothing less than spectacular, day and night. From its beautiful homes and views to its entertainment and cultural offerings, Brooklyn is red hot.

Big enough to be America's third-largest city, Brooklyn has enough attractions to fill an entire holiday. The borough is as ethnically diverse as Manhattan: Latinos from the Caribbean settled in Flatbush and Polish groups made Greenpoint their home. Italians and Chinese live predominantly in the Sunset Park area. Williamsburg has enclaves of Hispanics and Hasidic Jews, and just to the southeast is the largely African-American Bedford–Stuyvesant neighbourhood. There are so many Russians in Brighton Beach that it is known as Little Odessa.

GETTING THERE

You can get to Brooklyn in less than ten minutes on a subway from lower Manhattan, but to enjoy the vistas, opt to walk over or go by water taxi (❶ (212) 742 1969 Ⓦ www.nywatertaxi.com). The Gray Line hop-on, hop-off tour bus (see page 56) stops at several of Brooklyn's main attractions.

SIGHTS & ATTRACTIONS

Brooklyn Botanic Garden
The Japanese Garden, famous cherry blossoms and annual orchid show are just some of the highlights of the garden, which is home to 10,000 plant species. ⓐ 900 Washington Ave ❶ (718) 623 7200

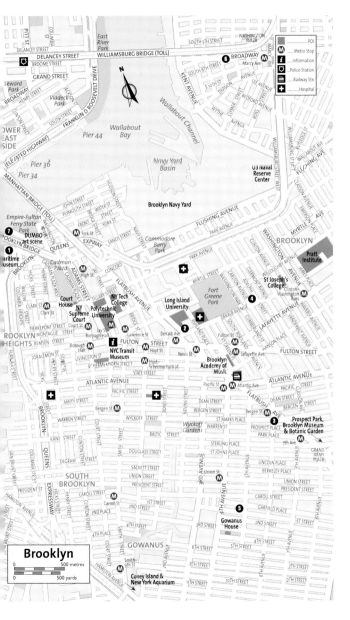

www.bbg.org 08.00–18.00 Tues–Fri, 10.00–18.00 Sat & Sun, closed Mon (14 Mar–5 Nov); 08.00–16.30 Tues–Fri, 10.00–16.30 Sat & Sun, closed Mon (6 Nov–13 Mar) Subway: 2, 3 to Eastern Parkway; B, Q to Prospect Park Admission charge

Brooklyn Heights promenade

Walk along the waterfront in Brooklyn Heights, the city's first designated historical district. You'll find sleepy streets and Greek Revival and Italianate row houses and it's also a great place from which to take in the city views. Subway: A, C to High St

Coney Island

The island that's really a peninsula swaggers on with more than a dash of seen-it-all charm. You haven't lived until you've witnessed (or participated in, or won) the Mermaid Parade beauty pageant. Subway: D, F, N, Q to Stillwell Ave

New York Aquarium

Sharks, penguins, walruses and sea otters – they're all here, alongside other marine life. Surf Ave & W 8th St (718) 265 3474 www.nyaquarium.com 10.00–17.00 Mon–Fri, 10.00–17.30 Sat & Sun (4 Apr–6 Sept); 10.00–18.00 Mon–Fri, 10.00–19.00 Sat & Sun (7 Sept–31 Oct); 10.00–16.00 (1 Nov–1 Apr) Subway: F, Q to W 8th St Admission charge

Prospect Park

Rivalling Manhattan's Central Park, Prospect Park's lush rolling landscape, with waterfalls and reflecting pools, offers visitors a carousel, an ice rink, the zoo and free summer concerts at the Bandshell. Grand Army Plaza, with its towering arch, marks the entrance to the park at Flatbush

Avenue and Eastern Parkway. Ⓦ www.prospectpark.org Ⓛ 05.00–01.00
Ⓜ Subway: 2, 3 to Grand Army Plaza; B, Q to Prospect Park

CULTURE

Brooklyn Academy of Music

BAM boasts a theatre and cinema, hosts the Brooklyn Philharmonic
and puts on the innovative Next Wave Festival. ⓐ 30 Lafayette Ave
Ⓣ (718) 636 4100 Ⓦ www.bam.org Ⓜ Subway: B, D, N, Q, R, 2, 3, 4, 5 to
Atlantic Ave–Pacific St; G to Fulton St; C to Lafayette Ave

🔺 *All the fun of the Coney Island fair*

⬥ *Cross the Brooklyn Bridge for the best views of Manhattan*

Brooklyn Museum

Home to 1.5 million items, including a renowned Egyptology collection and wonderful paintings by Edgar Degas, Georgia O'Keeffe and others.
ⓐ 200 Eastern Parkway ⓣ (718) 638 5000 ⓦ www.brooklynmuseum.org
ⓛ 10.00–17.00 Wed–Fri, 11.00–18.00 Sat & Sun, closed Mon & Tues
Ⓝ Subway: 2, 3 to Eastern Parkway–Brooklyn Museum
ⓘ Admission charge

DUMBO art scene

Emerging artists have taken over the cobblestone streets, and the gentrified area now has many boutiques, restaurants, art galleries and events. ⓐ 30 Washington St ⓣ (718) 694 0831
ⓦ www.dumboartscenter.org Ⓝ Subway: F to York St; A, C to High St

RETAIL THERAPY

If you want a break from the crowds in Manhattan, visit the boutiques and quirky stores in Brooklyn's neighbourhoods. In Park Slope, head to **Fifth Avenue**, roughly between Pacific Street and Ninth Avenue (Ⓝ Subway: B, D, F, N, Q, R, 2, 3, 4, 5 to Atlantic Ave–Pacific St). If you're in Carroll Gardens, walk along Smith and Court Streets, then check out **Atlantic Avenue** in Boerum Hill (Ⓝ Subway: F, G to Bergen St; A, C, E to Hoyt–Schermerhorn St). On Sundays in Fort Greene you'll find the **Brooklyn Flea**, a market with 200 vendors, on Lafayette between Clermont and Vanderbilt Avenues (🕐 10.00–17.00 Sun Ⓝ Subway: G to Fulton St). And don't miss out on hip **Williamsburg** (Ⓝ Subway: L to Lorimer St, G to Metropolitan Ave).

TAKING A BREAK

Brooklyn Ice Cream Factory £ ❶ Top up your calories with a double scoop here. Ⓐ Water St & Old Fulton St ❶ (718) 246 3963 🕐 12.00–23.00 Ⓝ Subway: A, C to High St

Junior's ££ ❷ Standard American fare like fried chicken and steak. An absolute must: their famous cheesecake. Ⓐ 386 Flatbush Ave EXT ❶ (718) 852 5257 ⓦ www.juniorscheesecake.com 🕐 06.30–24.00 Sun–Thur, 06.30–02.00 Fri & Sat Ⓝ Subway: B, Q, R to DeKalb Ave

AFTER DARK

If daytime Brooklyn's your scene, then you'll love immersing yourself in this atmospheric area's plethora of places to eat, drink and pose outrageously after hours.

RESTAURANTS

Flatbush Farm £ ❸ In the vanguard of the 'locavore' craze, the menu consists of organic, farm-fresh meats and, as often as possible, local produce and dairy products. ⓐ 76 Saint Marks Ave ❶ (718) 622 3276 ⓦ www.flatbushfarm.com ⓛ Restaurant: 17.30–23.00 Mon–Thur, 17.30–24.00 Fri & Sat, 10.30–15.30 Sun; Bar: 17.00– 02.00 Mon–Sat, 12.00–02.00 Sun ⓝ Subway: 2, 3 to Bergen St; B, Q to Seventh Ave

i-Shebeen Madiba £–££ ❹ Madiba is fashioned after the informal dining halls of South African townships, and the menu features stews and curries, among other treats. ⓐ 195 DeKalb Ave ❶ (718) 855 9190 ⓦ www.madibarestaurant.com ⓛ 16.00–24.00 ⓝ Subway: G to Clinton–Washington Aves

Blue Ribbon ££–£££ ❺ Known for its multi-ethnic menu and its child-friendly attitude. ⓐ 280 Fifth Ave ❶ (718) 840 0404 ⓦ www.blueribbonrestaurants.com ⓛ 17.00–24.00 Mon–Thur, 17.00–02.00 Fri, 16.00–02.00 Sat, 16.00–24.00 Sun ⓝ Subway: R to Union St

Peter Luger's £££ ❻ Prime beef and sizzling steaks that melt in your mouth. ⓐ 178 Broadway ❶ (718) 387 7400 ⓦ www.peterluger.com ⓛ 11.45–21.45 Mon–Thur, 11.45–22.45 Fri & Sat, 12.45–21.45 Sun ⓝ Subway: J, Z to Marcy Ave

River Café £££ ❼ Exudes romance and a fabulous view from the waterfront. ⓐ 1 Water St ❶ (718) 522 5200 ⓦ www.therivercafe.com ⓛ 12.00–15.00 & 18.00–23.00 Mon–Sat, 11.00–15.00 & 18.00–23.00 Sun ⓝ Subway: A, C to High St

ⓞ *The great atrium at famous Grand Central railway station*

PRACTICAL
information

Directory

GETTING THERE
By air

Large international airlines provide direct flights to New York and the Northeast Corridor from the UK. **British Airways** (W www.britishairways.com), **Virgin Atlantic Airways** (W www.virgin-atlantic.com) and **American Airlines** (W www.aa.com) fly from Heathrow with a dozen or so flights each day to John F Kennedy International Airport (see page 46) and Newark Liberty International Airport (see page 47). **Continental Airlines** (W www.continental.com) has several daily flights from Gatwick to Newark.

British Airways, Virgin and American Airlines also fly to Boston. BA goes to both Baltimore-Washington International (BWI) and Washington (Dulles). **United** (W www.united.com) and Virgin also fly to Washington (Dulles). Fares are pretty competitive on all these airlines, so you may choose the one you feel comfortable with. If you want to travel from Boston or Washington to New York by air, consider the frequent domestic flights that go into LaGuardia Airport (see page 47), which is closer to the city and a cheaper taxi ride. **US Airways** (W www.usairways.com) has a shuttle service every hour from Boston (⏱ 06.00–20.00), and from Washington, DC (⏱ 06.00–21.00, slightly reduced service at weekends). The Washington Shuttle leaves from Reagan National, close to the city's centre.

Many people are aware that air travel emits CO_2, which contributes to climate change. You may be interested in the possibility of lessening the environmental impact of your flight through the charity Climate

▶ *Subway trains are a fast way through the city*

Care, which offsets your CO_2 by funding environmental projects around the world. Visit Ⓦ www.jpmorganclimatecare.com

By rail

Travelling to New York by train is a pleasure. Amtrak's (see page 47) Acela Express leaves Union Station in Washington, DC and arrives at New York Penn Station 2 hours, 50 minutes later. Amtrak has a station at Baltimore-Washington International Airport, so if you're leaving from that area, it might be wise to fly into BWI in the first place; getting to Union Station from Dulles is a little more complicated.

From Boston's South Station, it's a three-and-a-half-hour train ride (on the same Acela Express), and you'll see all the New England states on your way to New York. The most obvious advantages of going by train are that it's usually punctual and that it takes far less time than buses and cars, which can get delayed in traffic and tunnels. The MBTA's **Silver Line** bus operates between Boston's South Station and Logan Airport.

By road

LimoLiner (Ⓞ (888) 546 5469 Ⓦ www.limoliner.com) is an innovative bus service from Boston to New York. This company wants its passengers to travel in a civilised fashion – leather bucket seats (only aisle or window), free fruit and cheese to munch on while surfing the net from a seat-side socket, and mobile phone reception – all this and four hours gets you to New York. **Washington Deluxe** (Ⓞ (866) 287 6932 Ⓦ www.washny.com) also has a premium service to New York, but without quite as many perks. Tried and trusted is **Greyhound** (Ⓞ (800) 231 2222 Ⓦ www.greyhound.com), which can get you to New York's Port Authority Terminal from just about anywhere in the US. The service to New York from Boston and Washington runs about once every hour.

Car-rental places are plentiful – just be sure to reserve ahead. Some savings can be had with a fly-drive package, but leave those four wheels far behind when you arrive in Manhattan. Avoid rush hours and late Sunday afternoon in summer.

ENTRY FORMALITIES

Most citizens of the UK, Ireland, Canada, New Zealand, Australia and Singapore with a valid machine-readable passport don't need a visa to visit the US for pleasure, on certain types of business, or in transit, if their stay will be for less than 90 days. This is part of the Visa Waiver Programme. Children must have their own separate machine-readable passports. Travellers must hold a return or onward ticket. If travelling on an electronic ticket, you will need a copy of the itinerary. You must also complete form I-94W, which is available from airline companies and will be offered to you on the flight. This form will require the address where you will be staying, including the zip code. All citizens will need a visa if they have been arrested, have a criminal record, or have a serious disease, including HIV. Citizens of Israel and South Africa must have visas to enter the US. It is advisable that the passport be renewed if it is valid for less than six months at the time of travel. For more information contact the **US Embassy** (ⓦ www.usembassy.org.uk).

Adults visiting the US are allowed one carton of cigarettes or 50 cigars, and a litre of liquor. They may also carry with them $100-worth of gifts, free of duty. Currency or monetary instruments worth over $10,000 are permitted but must be reported (coming in or going out). Customs forms to fill out are provided on inbound flights, so have your passport number handy.

Prescription medicine is permitted, but those containing narcotics require a statement or prescription from the patient's doctor for those particular drugs, and all medicines should be in clearly marked containers. Most foods, fruits, meats and plants are off limits, with few exceptions, so leave them behind. If you want to dig deeper into all the regulations, go to the **US Customs** website (Ⓦ www.customs.gov). On the way home, you'll have to comply with UK allowances, which are rather limited.

MONEY

The US dollar ($) is the basic unit of currency, divided into 100 cents. Paper bills come in denominations of $1, $2, $5, $10, $20, $50 and $100. The $2 bill is rarely seen, as they are traditionally kept as souvenirs. Even though these days a single dollar will hardly buy anything, coins are in regular use. There's a copper penny (1¢), silver-colour nickels (5¢), dimes (10¢), quarters (25¢), half-dollars (50¢) and a dollar coin, which is really easy to mistake for a quarter. Fortunately, the half-dollar and dollar coins are rarely seen. While the US treasury has remodelled various bills, they're still all the same size, so don't give away $100 when only $1 is due!

It is not a good idea to carry large amounts of cash, although if you're out clubbing for the night, cash may be the only option. Remember also that many smaller restaurants and cafés don't accept credit cards. Visa, MasterCard and American Express are the most recognised cards. Some shopkeepers and cashiers are wary about breaking the larger $50 and $100 bills, and taxi drivers don't have to change anything over $5.

Debit cards are widely accepted and the easiest for withdrawing money from your home bank. ATMs are everywhere, so consider this as an alternative to bringing large amounts of cash or traveller's

LOCAL LAWS

You must be aged 21 or over to buy or be served alcohol in New York, and you must be 18 to buy tobacco products. Restaurant and bar servers may ask for anyone's photo ID to verify age. If you drive, there is no right turn on red anywhere in New York City. Look for signs indicating special turn rules. You can be fined $50 if your mobile rings (and you are caught and cited) during theatre, concerts, films or the ballet, so remember to turn it off before the performance starts. The same rule applies in a public library.

cheques. If you choose to use traveller's cheques, buy them in smaller amounts up to $100. Banks in New York are open from 09.00 to 15.00 Monday to Friday, and sometimes later.

Note especially that prices are stated exclusive of sales tax. Expect to pay 8.375 per cent tax on almost everything, including restaurant and hotel bills, but not food bought in a grocery store, or clothes and shoe purchases under $110. Sales tax on goods purchased is administered by the state and no refunds are possible. Hotel rates have an additional tax as well.

HEALTH, SAFETY & CRIME

In any big city, especially one you don't know, it's better to be safe than sorry. That means being aware of what's going on around you. Keep cameras and handbags secure; they'll disappear without a trace if you lay them down while shopping. The ever-lowering crime rate is thanks to the vigilance of New York's recent mayors. It also has a lot to do with gentrification in every nook and cranny of Manhattan.

Places like the East Village, the Lower East Side, Alphabet City, Hell's Kitchen, Harlem and even Bed-Stuy (Bedford-Stuyvesant in Brooklyn), that once were termed 'Avoid at all cost!', are being rejuvenated with condos, boutiques and cafés.

New York police make safety a priority. They wear dark blue uniforms and can be very helpful. For what to do in an emergency, see page 154. Since 9/11, security checks are common in large buildings and in subway stations, so always carry a picture ID (preferably not your passport). For any incident involving the police, such as a theft, ask for a report.

New York water is clean and most people drink water from the tap. When crossing roads, remember that traffic drives on the right so be sure to look both ways before stepping off the kerb. Medical treatment in hospitals is prohibitively expensive in the US and it is essential that you carry comprehensive travel and medical insurance. At least $1 million coverage is recommended, to include hospital treatment and medical evacuation to the UK. Check the small print and exclusions, especially if you engage in sports. See page 154 for more information on medical emergencies.

OPENING HOURS

In the city that never sleeps it's difficult to pin down when things are open and when they are closed. Generally speaking, however, businesses are open 09.00 to 17.00 on weekdays. Banks are open at least 09.00 to 15.00 weekdays. Shops tend to open at 09.00 or 10.00 and close at 18.00 or later. Pharmacies and supermarkets are usually open by 08.00 and stay open late; some never close. Most **Duane Reade** pharmacies (Ⓦ www.duanereade.com) are open

NYPD car, ready to serve

24 hours a day. Major attractions and museums open by 09.00 or 10.00, and while many museums are closed at least one day of the week, they usually keep evening hours on one day.

TOILETS

New York's biggest mystery – what to do when you've got to go! There's actually a website to help solve this problem: cast an eye over Ⓦ www.nyrestroom.com. Luckily, most of the public libraries, bookshops, museums and large department stores have clean toilets. There are public toilets in various places in Central Park (see page 12), including in the zoo. Bars and hotels with large lobbies are good options, too. Additionally, the city installed its first public pay toilet in December 2007 near Madison Square Park (23rd St & Madison Ave), with at least 20 more planned for the future.

CHILDREN

It may be at odds with their preferred image, but New Yorkers love children. Hotels usually provide cots for babies at no additional charge. Supermarkets have whole aisles devoted to babies' and children's products such as nappies. Plenty of neighbourhood eateries are glad to serve the whole family, or you can try some of the many themed restaurants. Alternatively, just get a pizza – New York crusts are unsurpassed.

Children will love a trip on the River Hudson with Circle Line Cruises (see page 40). To make sure that idle hands don't create too much mischief, book some time at **Sony Wonder Tech Lab** (Ⓐ 56th St & Madison Ave Ⓣ (212) 833 8100 Ⓦ www.sonywondertechlab.com Ⓛ 10.00–17.00 Tues–Sat, 12.00–17.00 Sun, closed Mon), with its four floors of hands-on-electronic-everything. If you don't mind exposing

your offspring to more toys than they could possibly ever play with (but would still like), they'll love the indoor Ferris wheel at **Toys 'Я' Us** (⊡ 1514 Broadway ☏ (646) 366 8800 ⓦ www.toysrus.com ⏱ 10.00–22.00 Mon–Thur, 10.00–23.00 Fri & Sat, 10.00–21.00 Sun). Military life is made interesting at **Intrepid Sea-Air-Space Museum** (⊡ W 46th St ☏ (212) 245 0072 ⓦ www.intrepidmuseum.org), which includes a Navy Flight Simulator. The interactive games and exhibits at the **Children's Museum of Manhattan** (⊡ 212 W 83rd St ☏ (212) 721 1223 ⓦ www.cmom.org) will keep younger children intrigued for hours.

🔺 *Take the children on a Circle Line ferry*

Junior environmentalists can enjoy catch-and-release fishing for bass or sunfish at The Meer in Central Park (see page 12), where bamboo fishing poles are provided free. They're also sure to love feeding time at Central Park Zoo (see page 84).

❶ Make sure your child has his or her own passport.

COMMUNICATIONS
Internet
New York is wired. There's Wi-Fi Internet almost everywhere, even in many of the parks, including Union Square Park, Washington Square Park, Bryant Park and part of Central Park.

Phone
When making a long-distance telephone call, dial 1 before dialling the area code and number. In New York, you must dial 1 plus the city area code, even for local calls. For example, if you call the British Consulate in Manhattan, you dial (1) (212) 745 0200. Telephone codes for Manhattan are 212 and 646, and, in the boroughs, 718 and 347 are used. The code 917 is for mobile phones. Codes 800, 866, 877 and 888 are toll-free. A good general rule is never to dial out from a hotel room; you can find a public telephone in the hotel lobby, and dialling 800 numbers doesn't require a coin.

You will occasionally see letters instead of digits in phone numbers. The letters simply refer to the numbers on the keypad (#2 = ABC; #3 = DEF; #4 = GHI; #5 = JKL; #6 = MNO; #7 = PQRS; #8 = TUV; #9 = WXYZ).

Two useful numbers:

❶ 311 is New York City's call centre phone number for government information and non-emergency services.

TELEPHONING NEW YORK

To call the United States, enter your country's international dialling-out code (usually 00), followed by 1, followed by the city area code (see opposite), then the particular number you wish to call.

TELEPHONING ABROAD

To make international calls, dial 011, followed by the country code, followed by the number you wish to call (minus the initial 0). Some of the most used dialling codes are: Australia (61); Canada (1); New Zealand (64); South Africa (27); UK (44).

ⓘ 411 is used to obtain local Manhattan telephone numbers, usually a free call when made from a public telephone.

Post

Stamps can be obtained at local post offices, pharmacy vending machines and at newsstands. Dark blue postboxes are located on some street corners and all bear information about collection times. Express Mail arrives anywhere in the US by the next day, and takes about two to three days to the UK – but it needs a form and a trip to the post office. The city's main **Post Office** (🄴 441 Eighth Ave Ⓦ www.usps.com) is open 24 hours a day.

ELECTRICITY

Throughout the United States, electric current is 110–120V, 60Hz AC. US plugs have two flat pins. You can buy adaptors at the airport, in department stores and in hardware stores.

TRAVELLERS WITH DISABILITIES

Under both New York and federal law, facilities built after 1987 must provide access for people with disabilities. However, the city can still be difficult to negotiate. The **Mayor's Office for People with Disabilities** (❶ (212) 788 2830 Ⓦ www.nyc.gov/mopd) will send the book *Access New York* free of charge upon request by telephone. It has specific accessibility information for theatres, sports venues and more. The city's buses are equipped with lifts for wheelchair users – the going might be slow, but you can get anywhere in the city. Some, but not all, subway stations have lifts or ramps. All the major museums are accessible, as well as many of the galleries. Most hotels have specially fitted rooms for people with disabilities, and restaurants in hotels and their toilet facilities are properly equipped. The **Hands On!** organisation (Ⓦ www.handson.org) arranges sign language interpreting for many New York cultural events.

TOURIST INFORMATION

Tourist offices

New York City's Official Visitor Information Center ⓐ 810 Seventh Ave ❶ (212) 484 1222 Ⓦ www.nycgo.com Ⓛ 08.30–18.00 Mon–Fri, 08.30–17.00 Sat & Sun Ⓝ Subway: B, D, E to Seventh Ave; N, Q, R, S to 57th St; 1, 9 to 50th St

Information points

Brooklyn Tourism and Visitors Center ⓐ Borough Hall, 209 Joralemon St Ⓦ www.visitbrooklyn.org Ⓛ 10.00–18.00 Mon–Fri, closed Sat & Sun Ⓝ Subway: 2, 3, 4, 5 to Borough Hall; R to Court St; A, C, F to Jay St
Federal Hall Information Center ⓐ 26 Wall St Ⓛ 09.00–17.00 Mon–Fri, closed Sat, Sun & federal holidays Ⓝ Subway: J, Z to Broad St; 2, 3 to Wall St

NYC Heritage Tourism Center City Hall Park Park Row 09.00–18.00 Mon–Fri, 10.00–18.00 Sat & Sun Subway: 1, 2 to Park Pl; N, R, 4, 5, 6 to Brooklyn Bridge–City Hall; A, C to Broadway–Nassau St; E to World Trade Center; J, Z to Fulton St

Official Visitor Information Kiosk for Chinatown Junction of Canal & Walker Sts 10.00–18.00 Mon–Fri, 10.00–18.00 Sat & Sun Subway: J, N, Q, R, Z, 6 to Canal St

Many neighbourhoods have formed alliances and their websites give local information. A few are listed here:

Alliance for Downtown New York www.downtownny.com

The Bronx Tourism Council www.ilovethebronx.com

The Lesbian, Gay, Bisexual & Transgender Community Center www.gaycenter.org

Lincoln Square Business Improvement District www.lincolnbid.org

Lower East Side Business Improvement District www.lowereastsideny.com

Madison Avenue Business Improvement District www.madisonavenuebid.org

SoHoNYC.com www.sohonyc.com

Tribeca Organization www.tribeca.org

BACKGROUND READING

The Bonfire of the Vanities by Tom Wolfe. The author gives an authentic portrait of those who pound the pavements of the Upper East Side.

The Catcher in the Rye by J D Salinger. Another true-to-life New York setting for this classic.

The Emperor's Children by Claire Messud. Manhattan life leading up to 9/11, a film version is in the pipeline.

Emergencies

New York has two important 24-hour, free-call special-use numbers. ❶ 911 is for emergencies such as a serious accident or crime. If you need information about the emergency services (as opposed to needing the services themselves), phone ❶ 311.

MEDICAL SERVICES

If you have a medical emergency, dial ❶ 911 to request an ambulance. If an ambulance is not necessary, take a taxi to the nearest hospital. A list of physicians, clinics and hospitals is available through the **International Association for Medical Assistance to Travellers** (IAMAT, Ⓦ www.iamat.org). The association is free to join (they suggest a donation), and has a comprehensive directory of medical services and required immunisations. IAMAT's English-speaking doctors have reasonable set fees.

For minor ailments you can go to a clinic, which requires immediate payment but should be less costly than a hospital emergency room. DOCS Physicians/Beth Israel Medical Center (see below) has a walk-in clinic charging reasonable fees for primary care, but try to go early to avoid long waiting times. Some Duane Reade pharmacy locations (see page 146) have **DR Walk-In Medical Care** (Ⓦ www.drwalkin.com). TravelMD.com has a 24-hour **Urgent Care Center** (❶ (212) 737 1212), where patients are seen by appointment. It also provides in-hotel medical service through its physicians' and dentists' networks. Hospitals are located in nearly every neighbourhood. Some of the leading institutions are:

DOCS Physicians Walk-In Clinic/Beth Israel Medical Group Ⓐ 55 E 34th St ❶ (212) 252 6000

Mount Sinai Hospital Ⓐ 100th St & Madison Ave ❶ (212) 241 6500

St Luke's-Roosevelt Hospital ⓐ 1000 Tenth Ave ⓣ (212) 523 4000
TravelMD.com Urgent Care Center or **NY Hotel Urgent Medical Services** ⓐ 952 Fifth Ave ⓣ (212) 737 1212 ⓦ www.travelmd.com

POLICE

In case of a life-threatening emergency, you can dial ⓣ 911 from any telephone for free (see opposite). You can also dial ⓣ 0 to get operator assistance. If you need to contact the police for any other reason, such as theft, call ⓣ (636) 610 5000 for police information and to locate the nearest police precinct. If you make a report to the police, make sure you request a copy. If the nature of the problem is serious, be sure to let them know that you are a foreigner visiting the US and ask to speak with a consular officer of your home country.

EMBASSIES & CONSULATES

Australian Consulate ⓐ 150 E 42nd St ⓣ (212) 351 6500
ⓦ www.australianyc.org
British Consulate General ⓐ 845 Third Ave ⓣ (212) 745 0200
ⓕ (212) 745 3062 ⓦ www.britainusa.com/ny
Canadian Consulate ⓣ (212) 596 1628
ⓦ www.canadainternational.gc.ca
New Zealand Consulate ⓐ 222 E 41st St ⓣ (212) 832 4038
ⓦ www.nzembassy.com
Republic of Ireland ⓐ 345 Park Ave ⓣ (212) 319 2555
ⓦ www.consulateofirelandnewyork.com ⓔ congenny@aol.com
South Africa ⓐ 333 E 38th St ⓣ (212) 213 4880
ⓦ www.southafrica-newyork.net

Project editor: Jennifer Jahn
Layout: Trevor Double
Proofreaders: Jan McCann & Karolin Thomas

The publishers would like to thank the following individuals and organisations for supplying their copyright photographs for this book: Anna i Adria/diluvi.com, page 135; BigStockPhoto.com (Laura Clay-Ballard, page 141; Mike Liu, page 5; Mario Savoia, page 107); C R, page 25; Sergio Calleja, page 17; dreamstime (Eddie Toro, page 30); Gershwin Hotel, page 33; Getty Images (Gonzalo E Brea, page 21; Jeremy Edwards, page 97; Hiroyuki Matsumoto, page 89; Alex Hoggarth, page 13; Graham Hoggarth, page 27); Pascal Konings/Sxc.hu, page 29; Patrick Kwan, page 81; Dan McKay, page 19; Pictures Colour Library, pages 45, 65, 69; rollingrck, page 147; stu_spivack, page 82; Anita Theobald, pages 7, 15, 41, 57; William Warby, pages 139, 149; Randa Bishop, all others.

Send your thoughts to

books@thomascook.com

- **Found a great bar, club, shop or must-see sight that we don't feature?**
- **Like to tip us off about any information that needs a little updating?**
- **Want to tell us what you love about this handy little guidebook and more importantly how we can make it even handier?**

Then here's your chance to tell all! Send us ideas, discoveries and recommendations today and then look out for your valuable input in the next edition of this title.

Email the above address (stating the title) or write to: pocket guides Series Editor, Thomas Cook Publishing, PO Box 227, Coningsby Road, Peterborough PE3 8SB, UK.

WHAT'S IN YOUR GUIDEBOOK?

Independent authors Impartial up-to-date information from our travel experts who meticulously source local knowledge.

Experience Thomas Cook's 165 years in the travel industry and guidebook publishing enriches every word with expertise you can trust.

Travel know-how Thomas Cook has thousands of staff working around the globe, all living and breathing travel.

Editors Travel-publishing professionals, pulling everything together to craft a perfect blend of words, pictures, maps and design.

You, the traveller We deliver a practical, no-nonsense approach to information, geared to how you really use it.

shed
ands,
avel.

s our
crets
world,
th of
ravel.

yo
t trip
tage.

Thomas Cook pocket guides

PARIS

Your travelling companion since 1873

Thomas Cook